Consumer Behavior
Theories

Consumer Behavior Theories

Convergence of Divergent Perspectives with Applications to Marketing and Management

Rajagopal

BEP BUSINESS EXPERT PRESS

Consumer Behavior Theories: Convergence of Divergent Perspectives with Applications to Marketing and Management

First published in 2018 by
Business Expert Press, LLC
222 East 46th Street, New York, NY 10017
www.businessexpertpress.com

ISBN-13: 978-1-94744-114-9 (paperback)
ISBN-13: 978-1-94744-115-6 (e-book)

Business Expert Press Consumer Behavior Collection

Collection ISSN: 2163-9477 (print)
Collection ISSN: 2163-937X (electronic)

Cover and interior design by Exeter Premedia Services Private Ltd., Chennai, India

First edition: 2018

10 9 8 7 6 5 4 3 2 1

Printed in the United States of America.

With love to Arati, Ananya, and Amritanshu
who have always stood by my academic endeavors

Abstract

This book critically examines and analyzes the classical and neoclassical behavioral theories in reference to consumer decision making across the business cultures. The theoretical perspectives of consumer behavior have been explained in the book concerning changing marketplace environment and customer-centric business approaches followed by the multinational companies. The core discussions presented in this book highlight that the new theories can be derived based on the social values, business ambiance, and consumer attitudes to understand the consumer cognitive drivers meticulously and develop synergy with the business strategies. This book is divided into five chapters illustrated with the figures and examples that help readers to easily get the concept and approach of innovative business projects. Discussions in the book presents new insights on drawing contemporary interpretations to the behavioral theories of consumers, and guides the breakthrough strategies in managing the time, territory, target, and tasks pivoting around consumers and market competitiveness. The book illustrates the consumer analysis and market behavior mapping, and guides the companies to build sustainable businesses associating consumers in the competitive marketplace.

Keywords

behavioral theories, consumer behavior, decision-making, market competition, marketing strategies, multinational companies

Contents

Preface

Consumer psychology is complex, being asymmetric, and uncertain. It takes a long time to develop an attitude on any consumer perceptions. Building attitude in the marketplace is often impulsive than judgmental, and is largely determined by the pressure of consumer needs and available choices. Traditional consumption practice is often assimilated to the generic preferences of ethnic culture. There has been a sustained interest in ethnic consumers, developing composite cultural identities in emerged multicultural demographic contexts. The transitions among mainstream consumers and the local-global culture dichotomy are exposed to a wide diversity. The learnt, acquired, and shared consumption cultures among the range of local and global cultural demographics and markets deploy varied consumer attitudes. It is argued that shifts in consumer culture provide a stimulus to dynamic innovation in the arena of personal taste and consumption. Such dynamism in consumer preferences influences the cultural system, and is driven by continuous change in value and lifestyle. Therefore, the theories on consumer behavior need to be redefined and interpreted in a contemporary context to guide the companies toward making appropriate marketing decisions and customer-centric strategies.

Shopping behavior of consumers is also influenced by the attributes of social cognitive theory, which explains how variables such as self-regulation and self-efficacy direct the spending behavior and determine consumer lifestyles. Product attributes influence consumer perceptions of the personal relevance of a product or service to their needs, and the consumer preferences for product attributes are significantly linked to their lifestyle. Motivational forces are commonly accepted to have a key influencing role in the explanation of shopping behavior. Personal shopping motives, values, and perceived shopping alternatives are often considered independent inputs into a choice model. Consumer attitudes are an outgrowth of beliefs, feelings, and behavioral intentions toward any product and service. Perceptions of consumers may be developed for either branded or unbranded products displayed in a retail store. These components are dynamic in forming the attitude of consumers and can be viewed together since they are interdependent, and collectively represent forces that influence how the consumer will react to the object. Often consumers hold multiple beliefs that may range from positive to negative, and weigh them under the influence of peers and society. Beliefs that sustain in the minds of consumers, and are endorsed by the peers, society, and market players, construct attitude over a period. Now, various decision theories can be interpreted to understand the consumer behavior in context to the role of social theories of learning emerging from the bottom of the social behavior of consumers.

This book examines and emphasizes the classical and neoclassical behavioral theories in reference to consumer decision making across the business cultures, analyzing the changing marketplace environment to carry out customer-oriented strategies, and implement them carefully. One of the core arguments presented in this book is that the new theories can be derived based on the social values, business ambiance, and consumer attitudes to understand the consumer cognitive drivers meticulously and develop synergy with the business strategies. In the growing market competition in the 21st century, the corporate success depends on consumer-oriented business strategies by analyzing the right consumer psychology. However, it is evident from the failures of several corporate initiatives that companies are unable to manage business, as they cannot resolve the complexities in consumer behavior. This book presents new insights on drawing contemporary interpretations to the behavioral theories of consumers, and guides the breakthrough strategies in managing time, territory, target, and tasks pivoting around consumers and market competitiveness.

Understanding the emerging consumer behavioral perspectives helps companies toward developing manufacturing and operations dexterity, managing economies of scale, distribution, pricing, and promotion management. A new enterprise in the global marketplace needs strong management skills for consumer-driven strategies, competitiveness, and assuring sustainable growth. A fundamental challenge in interpreting the complexities associated with consumer behavior particularly in the large diversified marketplace depends on choosing the right analytical designs and interpreting desired outcomes.

This book is divided into five chapters illustrated with figures and examples that help readers to easily get the concept and approach of innovative business projects. Chapter 1 discusses the globalization effects on consumers and competitive differentiation to attract consumers, and analyzes consumer culture and markets in the changing global business perspectives. Discussions on current trend on generating consumer lifetime value by the multinational and local companies, and several arguments on the effects of consumerism due to shifting consumer economics and disruptive market tendencies, have been presented in the chapter. This chapter also presents a critical analysis of a wide range of business strategies used today by the multinational companies to reach low-end markets and inculcate cross-cultural consumer values. The arguments are supported by several examples of how new business models work in emerging markets and describe approaches for creating sustainable consumer lifetime value. Chapter 2 discusses consumer motivational, cognitive and physical, and consumer acquisition- and retention-related theories. Among others, the acquiescence effect, acquired needs theory, activation theory, affect infusion model, decision appraisal theory, attribution theory, Cannon–Bard theory of emotions, consistency theory, choice theory, cognitive appraisal theory, and conversion theory have been discussed in this chapter in the context of business impetus of companies. Besides discussion on the preceding theories, new routes to market for consumers and their implications on the business have also been presented in this chapter. The systematic discussion on the functions of decision metrics in competitive business is presented in Chapter 3, interpreting various decision theories. This chapter discusses selective decision theories including social learning and instructional learning theories, drive and cue theories, and optimal distinctiveness theory in the context of consumer behavior and managerial implications. Besides theoretical discussions, this chapter also discusses exogenous and endogenous elements affecting consumer cognition and behavior, convergence of stimuli and response of consumers, and critical indicators of consumer value and loyalty as drivers of consumer decision metrics.

Chapter 4 focuses on discussing the various perspectives of consumer behavioral patterns and performance appraisal in reference to relevant theories. Besides discussion on the shifting behavioral pattern of consumers today, this chapter discusses major personality theories encompassing Big-Five personality theory, psychoanalytic theory, cognitive bias, and theories of emotions. Management judgments, which managers follow concerning brands, products, and services, have been categorically discussed in this chapter. Among applied discussions on self-governing theories, this chapter also explains equity theory and expectancy theory in reference to contemporary business environment. The various cultural attributes like family, decision-making units, language, religion, and esthetics, which help companies in building behavioral brands, have been discussed in this chapter. The most functional topic on consumer behavior is discussed in Chapter 5, which critically examines various aspects of consumer involvement in the decision-making process. This chapter addresses anchoring or focalism, and four-factor model comprising arousal, behavioral control, emotions, and critical thinking as part of the judgmental theories. Various perspectives on behavioral filters over cognitive biasness, and aggressive and defensive behavior, have also been discussed in this chapter. Decision making among consumers is critical to market information. This chapter also discusses critically the causes and effects of information analytics on decision making along with the perspectives of brand personality and trust. The chapter concludes with the discussion on trends in consumer behavior.

The classical consumer theories have more philosophical than pragmatic orientation. Thus, most theoretical notions were knitted around the ethical perspectives. Ethical consumerism and family consumer decision making including the influence of children are the emerging spheres of consumer behavior as the globalization effect advances across the markets. In a family-led consumer decision, motivation to pursue an ethical lifestyle is an important attribute associated with an inheritance factor, where elder members of family are awakened to ethical issues. The consumerism today has turned materialistic, wherein value for money, value and lifestyle, and convenience appear to be the principal drivers governing the behavioral dimensions of consumers. Efficient management of stakeholders is the pivot to business growth in global-local competitive market dynamics. This book bridges the myths and realities on consumer behavior and suggests cost-effective and goal-oriented strategies for managing stakeholders. In today's dynamic and competitive world, a manager's key challenge is coping with frequent unexpected preferences of consumers and market demand. This book describes understanding and interpreting consumer behavior to offer the desired stakeholder value while carrying out business in the competitive marketplace.

Understanding consumer behavior is essential to support a set of key decisions that collectively determine how companies can perform in the competitive marketplace, manage costs and revenue, and mitigate consumer-led risks. This book argues about the new dimensions associated with the changing perspectives of consumer preferences, knowledge, values, and decision-making abilities as a driver for business growth and addresses several pertinent questions that include:

- What do consumer theories reveal?
- How to interpret consumer behavior in reference to contemporary market environment?
- Why should companies make business decisions based on the consumer experience?
- How to take a right consumer-led decision in business?
- Why do key decision makers need to drive the stakeholders' value?

This book provides the knowledge and skills that managers can use to develop consumer-driven strategies. Analysis of consumer behavior and business strategies have been explained systematically. Most growing companies have the vision to consistently create or introduce new business initiatives with customers and suppliers and incorporate consumer database into their enterprise resources planning systems. This book offers knowledge and skills also about developing the market-centric and competition-oriented models, and illustrates the power of consumers in managing sensitive market interventions through marketing-mix strategies, innovation, and technology application for expanding and establishing business in competitive markets. The book illustrates the consumer analysis and market behavior mapping, and guides the companies to build sustainable businesses associating consumers in the competitive marketplace.

The broad foundation of this book is laid on the conceptual discussions on consumer theories and applied arguments on shifts in consumer behavior. This book categorically reviews the project management theories, concepts, and previous researches, and discusses the applied tools and techniques for business projects. The book discusses contemporary project management approaches for the companies to grow competitive along with the market players and consumers. This book significantly contributes to the existing literature and serves as a learning post and a think tank for students, researchers, and business managers.

Rajagopal
October 20, 2017
Mexico City

Acknowledgments

In completing this volume of the book I have benefitted by the discussions of my colleagues within and outside the EGADE Business School. I am thankful to Dr. Tanya Zlateva, Dean of Metropolitan College, Boston University; Dr. John Sullivan, Administrative Sciences Department of Boston University; and Dr. Raquel Castaño, Professor and Director of EGADE Business School, Monterrey Campus, who have always encouraged me to take up new challenges in teaching graduate courses, develop new insights, and contribute to the existing literature prolifically. I thank all my students of graduate and doctoral programs at Boston University and EGADE Business School for sharing enriching ideas during the classroom discussions that helped in building this book on the framework of innovative ideas.

I also acknowledge the outstanding support of Robin J. Zwettler, Executive Editor of Business Expert Press, who critically examined the proposal, guided the manuscript preparation, and took the publication process forward. My special thanks are due to Dr. Naresh Malhotra, Regents Professor Emeritus at Scheller College of Business, Georgia Tech University, and series editor on consumer behavior subject at Business Expert Press, for his guidance and encouragement in bringing out this volume. I am thankful to various anonymous referees of my previous research works on innovation and technology management who helped in looking deeper into the conceptual gaps and improving the quality with their valuable comments.

Finally, I express my deep gratitude to my beloved wife Arati Rajagopal, who has been instrumental in completing this book like all other works of mine. I acknowledge her help in copy editing the first draft of the manuscript, and for staying in touch till the final proofs were cross-checked and index was developed.

CHAPTER 1

Exploring Consumers Today

Overview

Consumers of the 21st century have overcome the conventional value and turned to accept technology-driven marketing amenities. Digital space has offered higher transparency in business, and better opportunity for consumers to express their emotions across geo-demographic consumer segments. Shifts in wealth and income distributions of consumers, and shifts in corporate hierarchies at international and regional levels, have led to an escalation of consumer aspirations. This chapter discusses globalization effects on consumers, and competitive differentiation to attract consumers, and analyzes consumer culture and markets in the changing global business perspectives. Discussions on current trends in generating consumer lifetime value by the multinational and local companies and several arguments on the effects of consumerism due to the shifting consumer economics and disruptive market tendencies have been presented in the chapter. Discussion in this chapter also present a critical analysis of a wide range of business strategies being used today by the multinational companies to reach low-end markets and inculcate cross-cultural consumer values. The arguments in this chapter are supported by several examples of how new business models work in emerging markets, and describe approaches for creating sustainable consumer lifetime value.

Globalization and Consumerism

Conventional perspectives of globalization embed a mindset of allowing the flow of products and services of a company to the markets across the geo-demographic segments. This can be achieved using cross-border outlets to explore cost-effective opportunities, benefits, and costs in doing business. The core focus of companies today has turned consumer-centric, and the international companies are engaged in developing suitable strategy on how globalization can enhance existing products and profit formulas from international to bottom-of-the-pyramid market segments. However, organizations build their businesses on top of globalization by harnessing the most profitable strategies despite the behavioral differences across the markets and consumers. Such businesses display customer envelopment approaches, cocreate design and communications, harness the resources and competitive ideas, and aspire to achieve a global-local footprint to improve business performance and higher market competitiveness. Globalization has driven consumers toward working with the digital economy and virtual marketplaces. This trend enables most companies to establish real differentiators and best practices that can support managers in globalizing their businesses, ranging from tailoring the businesses for the local environment to leveraging global network effects (Kerr 2016). Various factors including continuous advancements in the information technology, social media communications, corporate initiatives to stay omnipresent in the global markets, and consumers' enthusiasm for digital commerce have significantly increased consumer openness in the global markets. The consumers are concerned today about the value, about the products that look attractive or stylish but are nonetheless significantly less expensive than traditional offerings. Customer-centric companies like Costco, H&M, IKEA, and Zara have attracted consumers around the world by offering combination of value and exciting shopping experience. Successful consumer companies like Amazon and Apple offer intuitive user experience to acquire and retain them, and turn the consumers brand loyal. Other companies, such as Walmart, use their global footprint and avoid a multilayered distribution system to introduce products at significantly lower prices.

Globalization trends among multinational companies are embedded in multilocation manufacturing, technological alliances, digital planning, and monitoring; evaluation systems in manufacturing and marketing; and focusing on e-commerce. Building a global company with circular manufacturing and marketing attributes needs new and nonconventional ways about managing organization, manufacturing, marketing, and developing a sustainable competitive strategy. The approaches that proved successful in the past include the experimentations of globalization with General

Electric Company (the United States), Toyota (Japan), Bosch (Germany), Cisco (the United States), and Haier (China). Most companies operating in the developed and emerging markets adopted best practices in the areas of lean manufacturing, operations management, logistics and inventory management, and customer relations management from these companies. However, replicating lean management practices of Japanese markets in various international and regional markets have outlived their experience. As the public safety concerns have mounted in the 21st century, governments of developing countries have become cautious of opening more industries to multinational companies. Besides, the rise of state capitalism in some emerging markets has altered the global playing field for companies (Bremmer 2014).

Current trends at the firm level suggest that globally integrated strategies toward manufacturing, operations management including logistics and inventory management, marketing, and innovation are oriented to attain first-mover advantage and stay ahead of competition for many industries. International business models explain industry trends from economic perspectives; and organizational excellence oriented toward attracting potential talents, managing business governance through technology, and developing strategies for setting an organic growth of the company over time and space. However, there is a gap in spatial business models in the area of strategic motivations of multinational firms, as they expand and integrate worldwide. Despite criticisms, companies should develop a capability-driven, as opposed to market-driven, framework to engross multinational strategy that could help companies to explore even the remote markets at the bottom of the pyramid. Such robust framework explains the organizational vigor for international expansion and global integration, depending on the capability types, capability strategies, and multinational strategies of the multinational firm (Tallman and Fladmoe-Lindquist 2002).

International consumer products companies are at edge of cocreating products today by commercialization of local innovations for wider markets. Godrej (India), General Electric (the United States), Nestle (Europe), and Unilever (the United Kingdom) have successfully experimented blending the local-global innovations, which may be identified as reverse innovation, to set their business roots in local markets. The emerging corporate-innovation model today is globally collaborative in reference to new product ideas, customer insights, business resources, and entrepreneurial intelligence coming from all over. For instance, more than 50 percent of innovation initiatives of Proctor & Gamble involve collaboration with outsiders. Innovations in the global marketplace have evolved from consumer needs to futuristic solutions. The evolution of markets over the centuries has been a perennial phenomenon congruent with the shifts in social, economic, and technological knowledge in the society. The evolution of business and growth has promoted economic behavior to explore the markets. Sociologically the evolution of markets was based on the understanding that individuals are embedded in various cognitive structures involving the business activities. Shifts in the market processes in the society are induced by fundamental beliefs and shared assumptions, and resemble elements of social culture defining norms of markets, expected behavior, and thought. Such business evolution paradigms are resistant to minor discrepancies between their fundamental models and contradicting (potentially empirical) evidence. Thus, discrepancies in market behavior are considered as socioeconomic abnormalities, paradoxes, or puzzles in a given place and time (Hedaa and Ritter 2005; Rajagopal 2012).

In the growing market competition, small firms always face major threat from large firms, as the latter possess more resources (physical, finance, human resources, and technology) than the smaller firms. Hence, most of the smaller firms develop cocooning attitude and confine to a niche, as they could not continue their struggle for existence in the marketplace. It may be observed that often large firms enter into new market niches created by small firms through technological innovation and ingest the market share of small firms. In view of the Darwinian Theory, it may be argued that market conditions and company-specific characteristics explain entry timing and underlying goals of the large firms. Such entry might be a continuous process for large firms in different marketplaces. The dominating behavior of large firms is more likely to be backed by the innovations in response to the competing firms. Small firms are affected by the entry of firms that are similar in size and resources. When a highly similar company enters the new market, it raises the probability that the company enters beyond levels based solely on the attractiveness of the market. Hence, small firms play aggressively and defensively to stay in the marketplace despite the competitive attacks by new entrants. On the contrary, consortium of small firms manufacturing identical products also poses a major threat to large firms in sustaining the competitive marketplace. For example, more than 20 companies have joined the Taiwan Blu-ray Disc (BD) Consortium, a special interest group, under the Taiwan Information Storage Association, formed by Taiwan-based companies involved in the BD market in 2010. The consortium includes makers of Blu-ray optical disc drives (such as Lite-On IT), optical discs (such as CMC Magnetics and Ritek), and integrated circuit design and components, hoping to join forces to negotiate better licensing terms for producing BD-related products. This consortium may cause a major threat to international BD manufacturers such as Sony to compete in the global marketplace against the consortium firms in reference to price and supply of BD products (Rajagopal 2012).

A good response to globalization was observed between 1980 and 2007. The economic recession in the United States during 2007–11 had raised several questions worldwide on the globalization, business performance, and public interests. The liberal trade routes, political agendas, and public diplomacy were conflicting with the globalization practices in the postrecession period. The myth of a borderless world has come crashing down after the referendum in 2016 about the coexistence of Briton with the European Union, and political ideology of the United States on globalization in 2017 changed with protectionist policies that have seriously affected the global trade. Traditional pillars of open markets such as the United States and the UK turned wobbling with their international business policies while China strengthened its opportunity in positioning itself as globalization's staunchest defender. In June 2016, the vote on Briton's exit from the European Union shocked the European Union, and the news coverage about globalization turned increasingly negative in the United States as the presidential election campaign progressed.

The concept of the global customer is gaining importance every day, and so is the global-customer-centric organization. The theory of comparative advantage suggests that firms may choose a destination to expand their marketing operation that offers relative economic advantage on factors of production (land, labor, and capital), technology, and managerial know-how. The comparative advantage in business may be defined as the ability of a firm to produce a specific good or service at a lower marginal and opportunity cost over another. Even if one country is more efficient in the production of all goods (absolute advantage in all goods) than the other, both countries will still gain by trading with each other, as long as they have different relative efficiencies. Going global is an easy process for firms. Firms need to simulate the impact of their business in global market in reference to their resources, target markets, and operational efficiency. Most firms concentrate on product markets considering the customers, who seek the same benefits or to be served with the same products, services, and innovation and technology regardless of the geo-demographic differences and cognitive behavior. There are a number of paradoxes in communicating the product-marketing strategies in global marketplace. For example, paradoxical values may emerge within and between cultures while advertising products and services in the global marketplace. It is necessary for the firms evolving to global scale to understand that markets are people, not products. There may be global products, but there are not global people; hence firms need to adopt the consumer-centric marketing approach in the global marketplace rather than going rampant in employing strategies to outmaneuver or outperform the competitors in the marketplace (Svensson 2012).

Continuous growth in innovation and technologies is the principal stimulants for the companies to gain competitive differentiation and attain leadership in the global markets, and to gain high brand equity to drive consumers toward new buying preferences and exploring new market segments. However, it is often hard for consumers to adopt innovations, gain confidence in deriving values appropriately, and derive competitive advantages from the innovative offerings over the existing and predetermined products and services. The consumer perceptions on the innovative products and technologies are largely influenced by the social and informal networks. Such interconnections among consumers and companies are so strong that often a new product's adoption by one player depends on its systematic adoption by other players. Globalization and the need for omnipresence have driven bidirectional impetus in the 21st century among the companies to have the global-local posture in business endeavors. Consequently, the multinational companies are thriving to make their place in the bottom-of-the-pyramid market segments, and expand their outreach in the mass markets, while the local companies are exploring the opportunities to grow global. Thus, every company is engaged in mapping the comparative advantages over the factors of production comprising land, labor, capital, technology, and managerial know-how across the potential destinations. Companies choose to move their production and business operations in the destinations that offer a potential advantage on the costs associated with the factors of production.

The market driver is considered as one of the strongest forces that push the process of global marketing. The *market driver* comprises the needs of local customers, global customers, global channels, and transferable marketing. The common customers' needs become a compelling factor for the multinational companies, when customers of different countries have the same needs in a product category. Free trade and unrestricted travel have created homogenous groups of customers across countries in reference to specific industries. However, some markets that typically deal with the culture-bound products like food and beverages, apparel, and entertainment strongly resist the shift toward globalization and remain multidomestic. On the contrary, global customers need the same products or services like Eastman Kodak Company or Hilton Hotels in many countries. The global distribution channels and logistics companies offer seamless transport, storage, and delivery services. A firm can expand internationally, provided the channel infrastructure meets the distribution needs of the company. Hence, the integrated networks thrive to bring multinational companies close to the global distributors and retail stores like supermarkets and departmental stores in order to generate systems effect. Celebrity endorsement is applied to impulsive social marketing ideas on brand names, packaging, advertising, and other components of marketing mix in different countries. Nike's campaign anchoring the basketball champion Michael Jordan improved the brand in many countries. This is how the good ideas of multinationals get leveraged world over.

Competitive Differentiation

Continuous increase in the competition at global marketplace has prompted companies to develop strategies for competitive differentiation in order to create customer value and achieve sustainable business performance. Companies introduce differentiation in product attributes, use value, complementarity, pricing, innovation and technology, digital marketing strategies, social media communications, and product promotions. Most companies in the emerging markets engage in continuous innovation and technology upgradation of products and services. Innovative companies adopt competitive strategies by understanding fundamentally new market space and consumer segments by creating products or services, for which there are no direct competitors. In developing competitive differentiation, most customer-centric companies cocreate an innovative value by blending the innovation, customer value, and competitive differentiation attributed in their products and services. Such value innovation creates a different competitive mindset among consumers, and a systematic way of looking for opportunities for the companies. Instead of looking around the conventional boundaries that define the competition within industry, companies tend to develop strategies to stay sustainable and acquire customers. By doing so, companies mark their business territories, earn loyal customers, and try to gain first-mover advantages that offer real value to innovation and product differentiation.

Customers always tend to make a trade-off between substitute products and the products of original innovation that offer sustainable value. Home Depot, for example, looked across the several substitutes of energy products, and launched its low-cost small energy-saving bulb brand, serving home improvement needs. In current times, this store brand is competing with Philips and GE energy brands. Companies develop their strategies using emotional psychodynamics to grow their private brands and attract consumers (Kim and Mauborgne 1999). Most emerging companies find continuous innovation challenging, and maintain competitive differentiation. However, watching consumer preferences across geo-demographic segments helps companies to develop appropriate strategies and strengths to stay competitive in the marketplace. Companies engaged in delivering low-cost innovations at low prices are often susceptible to disruptive products and low-cost competitors that create defection among consumers. Many price leaders in the mass consumer market, such as Walmart, are also changing the nature of competition by employing competitive differentiation in products and services, and educating consumers about their right and sustainable choices. Price competitors are focusing on few consumer segments by delivering innovative products, and enhancing higher customer value. As the globalization is growing bidirectional today, local enterprises are surging to reach cross-market consumer segments, and large multinational companies are protecting their market against the low-price rivals. Competitive differentiation includes new product attributes, enhanced complementarity, higher perceived use value, extended product life cycle, operations efficiency, and omnipresence of the products and services. Low-price innovations are not an answer for the competitive differentiation. Most companies take various approaches to differentiate their products using local enterprise collaborations, commercializing reverse innovation, and growing sustainable in the marketplace catering to all consumer segments.

Companies that are grown on the small resources and local business environment consider launching low-cost businesses as a competitive differentiation strategy, as many low-cost airlines founded their business with low price-limited service premises since the 1990s in the American, European, and Asian markets. Some companies that adopted dual strategy converging innovation and customer value experienced competitive differentiation, which has generated synergies between their existing businesses and the new ventures. Ryanair in Europe sustained in aviation business as a low-cost airline, and caught attraction of the industry as a radical marketing airline for its proposal to introduce standing passengers for flight shorter than 45 minutes. The competitive differentiation strategies go well with both low-cost and value-added players (Kumar 2006).

A large number of companies in emerging markets have managed to develop competitive differentiation to stay ahead of multinational companies. Local companies customize products and services to meet ethnic consumer needs and slowly follow the economies of scale. Small emerging companies develop business models to overcome market-specific difficulties and attempt to gain competitive advantage against the multinational brands in the marketplace over the time. However, consumers prefer to stay with the companies that deliver products and services with the latest technologies and augment competitive advantage. Regional companies gain price leadership quickly as they find ways to support a low-price strategy through the low-cost labor, and offering in-house training to their employees in lieu of hiring skilled employees, which escalates costs. However, they invest in top management talent in order to drive rapid growth. Successful homegrown champions that have grown global, such as Yum Brands, Nokia, and Hyundai, have managed to overturn the local competitors by using the previous organizational and marketing management strategies (Bhattacharya and Michael 2008).

Most companies manage market competition, shifts in technology, or new customer demands by taking consumers into confidence in order to ensure compatibility of business model and corporate strategies. Successful companies in rapidly changing, intensely competitive industries take a co-design and systematic change approach as well to create competitive differentiation, and enhance consumer value periodically. Multinational companies change manufacturing, marketing, and services strategies proactively through regular deadlines as competitive pacing tool. Appropriate pacing of marketing strategies to match market competition should be synchronized with the value, speed of implementation, and extent of consumer benefits. For example, 3M accounts for one-fourth of its revenues every year from new products, Samsung introduces a new consumer electronics product about every two quarters, and Intel adds a new fabrication facility to its operations approximately every nine months. Time pacing to match market competition is a continuous process that creates a relentless sense of urgency to stay ahead of competition and become market leader. Companies such as Cisco Systems, Dell Computer, Intel, Kellogg's, Nintendo, and Unilever implement strategies to manage market transitions toward consumer preferences, new product development, and gaining first-mover advantage. Companies that are successful in time pacing in market competition build business dynamics and manage transitions effectively by delivering desired consumer values (Eisenhardt and Brown 1998).

Emerging markets such as China and India have become the strong market competitors to the multinational companies from rest of the world. The regional growth drivers of these Asian countries have been very powerful that encouraged manufacturing products of international standards at local level and achieved the price leadership. Indian and Chinese companies are shifting their innovation focus from cost saving to knowledge-based research to compete with multinational companies. However, Indian and Chinese multinationals have not geared up to move at the desired pace with international competitors. Hence, they have been at a competitive disadvantage, particularly in strategic technology industries. These companies still need to improve their strategies to overcome consumer perceptional barriers to accept the strategically important technology industries, in which "Made in China" or "Designed in China" are viewed as negatives. Some companies are on war to improve their strategies, and gain international recognition to their brands. Huawei, a Chinese telecommunication technology company, has improved its marketing strategy to deliver better consumer value by offering customized technologies that meet the practical needs and resource constraints of target customers, and build customer loyalty by enhancing practical innovation with longer-term joint innovation partnerships (Hensmans 2017). Consumers value differentiation, and create opportunities for companies to improve their performance in existing markets or break into new markets. The competitive differentiation in products and services helps companies to develop stronger customer loyalty, greater consumer willingness to try a particular brand, and sustained revenue growth. In order to create sustainable competitive differentiation, companies should arrange the elements of differentiation in a pyramid according to functional needs, emotional drivers, quality of life index, and social impact of new products (Almquist, Senior, and Bloch 2016).

Consumer Culture and Markets

Globalization has catalyzed the growth of fashion industry, and the marketplace attractions have driven the cultural attributes of consumers significantly across various consumer segments. Shifts in the cultural values, consumer preferences, and purchase intentions toward designer products are arguably the most critical issues faced by the marketing managers today. Many researchers argue that the increasing globalization is reducing the homogeneity of consumer behaviors within countries, while increasing communalities across countries (Cleveland and Laroche 2007). Most firms manufacturing designer apparel are trying to bridge intercultural differences and building cultural consonance across consumer segments on a variety of contexts that stimulate interest in fashion apparel. Firms use a customer-centric market strategy developed on self-esteem attributes of consumers to enhance purchase intentions toward fashion apparel (Horowitz 2009).

The marketplace in the 21st century has become more complex than before because of increasing competition, shifts in consumer preferences, and corporate governance practices. Companies have turned customer centric, and consider customer as the focus of developing marketing strategies for business growth. Consumer behavior is getting multifaceted in the global marketplace due to rapid increase in competition, innovation, and technology in products and services. Hence, architecting sustainable companies is not getting any easier. A longitudinal growth of brands across the companies has altered the perception, attitude, and behavior of consumers rapidly over time. Thus, companies are engaging consumers in building confidence on brands and the company by developing a symbiotic relationship between consumers and market for sustainable growth. Companies build consumer perceptions on the product and services by disseminating continuous and sustainable communication through various cable channels to the Internet, product placement in movies, and even mobile-phone display screens. The first order of business is to take a hard look at the sustainable consumer segment that has the long-term profit potential for delivering right brands for segments, and to plan for required investment in building the customer-centric markets. While no good company ignores shifts that are clearly under way, it traditionally segments markets in reference to the size, income, age, and ethnicity of various target populations; estimates of their consumption and loyalty; and information about their locations, lifestyles, needs, and attitudes. Well-managed companies have moved from emphasizing on customized items to offering globally standardized products that are advanced, functional, reliable, and low priced. They benefit from enormous economies of scale in production, distribution, marketing, and management. Such dynamism in the business and related activities portrays the functional concepts of globalization (Rajagopal 2008).

Powerful market stimulants such as fashion shows on television, fashion advertisements, in-store displays, and fashion events in the urban shopping malls have influenced the transnational cosmopolitanism among consumers. Such interactive marketing strategies of fashion apparel have shown convergence of traditional and modern values and lifestyle to develop a homogeneous global consumer culture. The conventional method of using societal icons as the cultural drivers has now been replaced by global fashion players with flagship brands as a basis for product position and market segmentation. It is found that multichannel systems of brand building and differentiation influence the consumers toward fashion apparel, and need is created at local levels supportive of, and constituted by, cultural industries. Milan, a city in Italy has become a destination brand for fashion design companies to exhibit their products through various media channels (Jansson and Power 2010).

Consumption has often been dichotomized in terms of its functional-hedonic nature and is closely associated with the level of satisfaction leading to determine the customer value influence (Wakefield and Inman 2003). As new products are introduced, a firm may routinely pass these costs on to consumers, resulting into high prices. However, a less obvious strategy in a competitive situation may be to maintain price, in order to drive the new product in the market with more emphasis on quality, brand name, postsales services, and customer relations management as nonprice factors. Many studies advocate value based customer relationship models for acquiring new customers and retaining loyal customers. Most importantly, the approaches suggested in these studies are expected to rise their spending and association with the products and services of the company with increasing levels of consumer satisfaction (Reichheld and Sasser 1990). In a marketing environment of a firm, a brand should be grown by studying the conditions under which it is expected to sustain. There are various factors that affect the management of a brand:

- Social and cultural factors
- Market competition-related factors
- Consumer perceptions
- Economic factors related to business and consumers

Companies need to understand the factors that drive consumer stimuli toward getting associated with new products and brands. The cognitive drivers that affect consumer behavior are as discussed as follows:

- Social status to acquire and use specific products
- Self-esteem and personality enhancement
- To make contribution to the society and business by service as lead user and brand ambassador
- To satisfy hedonic value and self-governance
- To stay in public domain and gain social prominence by getting involved in the green products and with eco-friendly companies

These factors help companies to develop consumer behavior as well as manage related business environments to develop a marketing strategy and inculcate consumer behavior. An understanding of environment helps the managers to assess the extent of the investment required to strengthen the brand, and develop strategies accordingly. Conditions of brand environment provide a base for formulating the developing brand policy and its measurement to provide magnitude and direction categorically to the brands of a company.

It has been observed that cultural values affect the purchase intentions of consumers across the market segments. In the societies that exhibit hedonic values, fashion apparel is promoted by manufacturers and retailers to induce a sudden, compelling, socially complex buying behavior through the promotional programs, to increase disposable income by facilitating credit to consumers (Venkatesh et al. 2010). Manufacturers and retailers apply both push and pull strategies to make the promotions of brands effective and advantageous to the consumers. Promotions targeted at final consumers, known as pull promotions, directly offer extra value to consumers, with the primary goals of attracting consumers to retail locations, and stimulating immediate sales. Though both push and pull promotions are designed to speed up the selling process and increase sales, at least in the short term, their strategic implications as well as their impacts on product sales and profits are believed to be different. Such a promotion-led retailing culture stimulates fashion-oriented attitudes, debt, and spending behavior on clothing, among consumers (Martin-Herran, Sigue, and Zaccour 2010).

Consumer culture varies across the markets and geo-demographic segments. Consumers in Asia, different regions of Europe, Africa, Pacific, and Americas have different attributes, which need to be carefully investigated by the companies to develop consumer-centric marketing strategies. Companies deploy significant resources for a deeper understanding of the important role played by the diverse consumer culture in the global marketplace of the 21st century. Asian consumer culture is not a coherent knowledge tradition, largely influenced by the collectivism or Confucianism philosophies; and it drives the consumer behavior socially rather than with individualistic concerns. The convergence of cultural traditions, characterized by social differentiation and complexity, demands various transformations in business strategies that could inculcate new trends and choices among the consumers in the Asian region and beyond (Seo and Fam 2015). Chinese consumer culture has distractive features, and it comprehensively represents conventional typologies like collectivism-individualism. However, contemporary culture in China is rapidly changing, breaking away from traditions. Most consumers are converging core traditional values with modern trends, and reshaping them sometimes with the alien inputs. The consumption behavior of millennials in China is motivated and orchestrated by capitalistic and materialistic societal development that has driven the Chinese consumers to adapt to the Western consumption trends and business practices (Piron 2006).

Retailers have adopted customization approach to successfully market a wide range of designer products, such as eyeglasses, bicycles, coffee, greeting cards, and apparel. The intention of purchasing of designer products differs across cultures. Customer preference and value placed on designer apparel are largely influenced by the social differentiation of products and self-esteem of the consumers (Moon, Chadee, and Tikoo 2008). These attributes are likely to vary depending on the customers' cultural orientation. The cultural dimensions of individualism, uncertainty avoidance, power distance, and masculinity should be a useful framework to explain cross-cultural differences in customer acceptance of designer products. Consumers use destination brands for their symbolic value, reflecting the personality and status of the user. Destination brands are perceived as an ostentatious display of wealth. Thus, consumers are motivated by the desire to impress others with their ability to pay high prices for prestigious products (Rajagopal 2011). Such personality dimensions often play a critical role in shifting the consumer culture toward brand-led buying behavior of utilitarian goods. The competitively differentiated brands are perceived by the consumers as prestigious brands encompassing several physical and psychological values such as perceived conspicuous value, perceived unique value, perceived social value, perceived hedonic value, and perceived quality value (Prendergast and Wong 2003). Consumption patterns are largely governed by social value of the product, which determines the purchasing intentions, consumer attitudes, or perceptions on brand or advertising slogan. Consumer experience with high socio-economic power perceptions creates qualitatively distinct psychological motives toward new products that develop unique consumption patterns (Rucker and Galinsky 2009).

Manufacturers and marketers develop their strategies through four processes in order to induce change in the consumer culture. These include chartering, learning, mobilizing, and realigning that pave the way for successful institutionalization of a strategic change initiative. The elements rely on an understanding of the mix of task-related, emotional, and behavioral factors in today's metrics-driven environment. This also drives the shift in conventional wisdom about programmatic change, arguing that managers need to set in motion, a series of processes right at the start if widespread changes are to stick (Roberto and Levesque 2005). The cultural change in buying apparel from low-price brands to designer brands in emerging markets has been institutionalized in a family environment. It has been observed that parental and sibling influences decrease with age, whereas peer and media influences expand with increasing age. The television and celebrities also play a significant role in influencing adolescents' clothing choices, irrespective of gender categories. Among the two most common forms of media children largely use are magazines and television, while teens are primarily influenced by visual merchandising, hands on experience, and spotting the fashion apparel users (Seock and Bailey 2009).

Diverse patterns of consumption create a consumption behavior that can be described extemporaneous, expedient, and emergent behavior. The nature of the consumption process depends on a host environment, and the drivers influencing the consumption pattern. These drivers include culturally diverse decisions of the consumer, multicultural identities, social cues, contextual factors, and tendency of consumers toward experimentalism. Consumers living in a frequently changing social and cultural environment across the geo-demographic segments become culturally plural, and turn experimentalists. Accordingly, the learning process among consumers stretches beyond boundaries, and becomes adjustable to the current state of sociocultural diversities (Sankaran and Demongeot 2011). Purchase intensions among the consumers are built by the companies using AATAR tactics and strategies as discussed in the following:

- Awareness: outreach and frequency of communication, clarity of communication, endorsements on quality and social value of the product by professional associations and celebrities, community education, brand literacy, and peer influence
- Attributes: competitive advantages on features of the product, innovation and technology components in the product, sustainable and extended life cycle of products, and high product attractiveness
- Trial: product experimentation, adaptability, and perceived use value
- Availability: route to market, convenience to customer, and store ambiance
- Repeat buying: brand confidence and loyalty

Brand personality and consumer inclination toward a brand are also developed through the celebrity connections and meanings of brand names. According to the theory of meaning (Smedslund 2011), symbolic properties of the celebrity first become associated with the brands the celebrity endorses. Next, these symbolic meanings are transferred from the celebrity to consumers as they select brands with meanings congruent with their self-concept. When the symbolic properties associated with brands, via celebrities, are used to construct the self, or to communicate the self-concept to others, a self-brand connection is formed. A consumer may appropriate symbolic brand meaning derived from a celebrity, who has characteristics the consumer aspires to possess. Therefore, the activation of self-enhancement goals by a threat to the self should increase the extent to which celebrity endorsement influences self-brand connections. It is argued in some research studies that celebrity-based brand associations can help consumers achieve goals that are motivated by the self, when celebrity-based brand associations are linked or connected to the individual preferences. Consumer involvement in brand develops possessive behavior and consumption culture not only with individuals, but also among the peers. Possessions can be used to satisfy psychological needs, such as actively creating consumer's self-concept, reinforcing and expressing self-identity, allowing one to differentiate oneself, and asserting one's individuality. Possessions can also serve a social purpose by reflecting social ties to family, community, and cultural groups, including brand communities (Rajagopal 2012).

Consumer Lifetime Value

Consumer lifetime value (CLV) is a key metric within consumer relationship management. Although, a large number of marketing scientists and practitioners argue in favor of this metric, there are only a few studies that consider the predictive modeling of CLV. This chapter focuses on the prediction of CLV in consumer goods manufacturing and marketing firms. In these industries, consumer behavior is rather complex, because consumers can purchase more than one service, and these purchases are often not independent from each other (Donkers, Verhoef, and Martijn 2003). However, it has been observed that low perceived use value, comparative advantages over physical attributes, and economic gains of the product make a significant impact on determining the consumer value for relatively new products. The consumer value gap may be defined as the negative driver that lowers the returns on the aggregate consumer value. This is an important variable, which needs to be carefully examined by a firm, and its impact on the profitability of the firm needs to be measured in reference to spatial (coverage of the market) and temporal (over time) market dimension (Marjolein and Verspagen 1999).

One of the principal drivers of consumer behavior is the dominance of social interactions. The involvement of consumers' products depends not only on their own perceptions but also on peers' response to their personality and change proneness (Pinheiro 2008). The relation between clothes and identity is perceived by consumers from the perspective of their values generated in various social interactions. Consumers get involved in exhibiting lifestyle as an esthetic way of presenting their personality. Hence, clothing is often considered as an opportunity for communicating a new order of identity of a person. In this process, there are both cognitive and affective incentives that translate into potential welfare gains (or indifference) for the consumers in a given social and work-related environment (Bianchi 2002).

Contemporary researchers have emphasized that, toward maximizing the lifetime value of consumers, a firm must manage consumer relationships for the long term. In disagreement to this notion, a study demonstrates that firm profits in competitive environments are maximized when managers focus on the short term with respect to their consumers (Villanueva et al. 2004). Intuitively, while a long-term focus yields more loyal consumers, it sharpens short-term competition to gain and keep consumers to such an extent, that the overall firm profits are lower than, when managers focus on the short term. Further, a short-term focus continues to deliver higher profits even when consumer loyalty yields a higher share of wallet, or reduced costs of service, from the perspective of the firm. Such revenue enhancement or cost reduction effects lead to even more intense competition to gain and keep consumers in the short term. The findings of the study suggest that the competitive implications of a switch to a long-term consumer focus must be carefully examined before such a switch is advocated or implemented. Paradoxically, CLV is maximized, when managers focus on the short-term benefits for consumers.

The role of customer value has been largely recognized by the firms as an instrument toward stimulating market share and profit optimization. The customer values for a new product of a firm in competitive markets are shaped more by habits, reinforcement effects, and situational influences than strongly held attitudes. The customer value is an intangible factor, which has a significant role in influencing the buying decisions. The customer value broadly includes psychometric variables like brand name, loyalty, satisfaction, and referral opinions. The consumer lifetime value is built over time by the business firms, which also contributes to the individual perceptions of the customers and augments their value.

In the growing competitive markets, the large and reputed firms are developing strategies to move into the provision of innovative combinations of products and services as "high-value integrated solutions" tailored to each consumer's needs than simply "moving downstream" into services. Such firms are developing innovative combinations of service capabilities, such as operations, business consultancy, and finance, required to provide complete solutions to each consumer's needs in order to augment the consumer value toward the innovative or new products. It has been argued that the provision of integrated solutions is attracting firms traditionally based in manufacturing and services, to occupy a new base in the value stream centered on "systems integration" using internal or external sources of product designing, supply, and consumer-focused promotion (Davies 2004). Besides the organizational perspectives of enhancing the consumer value, the functional variables like pricing play a significant role in developing the consumer perceptions toward the new products. The key marketing variables such as price, brand name, and product attributes affect consumers' judgment processes, and derive inference on their quality dimensions leading to consumer satisfaction. An experimental study conducted indicates that consumers use price and brand name differently to judge the quality dimensions and measure the degree of satisfaction (Brucks, Zeithaml, and Naylor 2000). The value of corporate brand endorsement across different products and product lines, and at lower levels of the brand hierarchy, also needs to be assessed as a consumer value driver. Use of corporate brand endorsement, either as a name identifier or as logo, identifies the product with the company, and provides reassurance for the consumer (Rajagopal and Sanchez 2004).

The analysis of the perceived values of consumers toward new products is a complex issue. Despite considerable research in the field of measuring consumer values in the recent past, it is still not clear how value interacts with marketing-related constructs. However, a comprehensive application model determining the interrelationship between consumer satisfaction and consumer value is needed, which may help in reducing the ambiguities surrounding both concepts. A systematic analysis of customer value in the previous studies indicates convergence of the following values:

- Perceived values
- Cultural values
- Personal values
- Consumption values
- Esthetic and hedonic values
- Social and family values
- Purchase convenience and postpurchase values
- Monetary values

Improving consumer value through faster response times for new products is a significant way to gain competitive advantage. In the globalization process, many approaches to new product development emerge, which exhibit an internal focus, and view the new product development process as terminating with product launch.

Companies today create consumer value by driving consumers toward destination brands, which embed cross-cultural emotions and ethnicity. Some companies like Apple, Samsung, and Cadbury's are routinely testing innovations with rich consumer-transaction data within cultural and ethnic diversities. Introducing a random change in the consumer culture has become a radical approach to inculcate new values among consumers. The digital space, such as websites, commercial blogs, and social media platforms including Facebook, is being extensively used to mitigate consumer anomalies in adapting to new consumer culture and adapting modern values of consumption. Most companies that adopt a *test and learn* culture to promote new trends tend to realize the greatest benefits by stimulating consumers to stay along vogue, and gain enhanced consumer values. Commonly, tactical decisions such as choosing a new store format and recreational retaining strategies of companies attract consumers to set in the new value trends (Davenport 2009).

Customer satisfaction includes location convenience, one-stop shopping convenience, firm reputation, firm expertise, and direct mailings on both customer retention and cross-buying. Trust and satisfaction play different mediating roles in the relationships between service attributes, customer retention, and cross-buying (Liu and Wu 2007). Relationship value is an antecedent to relationship quality and behavioral outcomes, and displays a stronger impact on satisfaction than on commitment and trust. Value also directly affects a customer's intention to expand business with a supplier. In turn, its impact on the propensity to leave a relationship is mediated by relationship quality (Voss et al. 2005). Value of relationship with the customer reveals significant quality and behavioral outcomes in the sales activities. Value displays a stronger impact on satisfaction than on commitment and trust, and directly affects a customer's intention to expand business with the firm. Perceived strength of the relationship with the customers may be measured by salespeople in reference to technical ability, experience, pricing requirements, speed of response, frequency of customer contact, degree of cooperation, trust, length of relationship, friendship, and management of distance barriers (Rajagopal 2009).

The modern market has emerged with the announcement that ethnic dressing comes from the core of the traditional culture whose gorgeous fabrics have been facelifted as convenience apparel within societal value and lifestyle (VALS) system. It is argued that shifts in consumer culture provide a stimulus to dynamic innovation in the arena of personal taste and consumption. Such dynamism in consumer preferences is considered as part of an international cultural system and is driven by continuous change in VALS. The consumer values like functionality, fitness for purpose, and efficiency significantly contribute in driving cultural change and recognizing suitable lifestyles (Hartley and Montgomery 2009). The growing technology-led apparel selling is one of the major stimulants for inducing change in fashion and consumer culture. The three-dimensional automatic made-to-measure scheme for apparel products, demonstrated through computer simulation in large departmental stores and lifestyle centers, play a major role in creating cognitive arousal among consumers. The apparel designers, manufacturers, and retailers, to represent the complex geometry models of apparel products, adopt a freeform design platform. Apparel products are essentially designed with reference to human body features, and thus share a common set of features as the human model. Therefore, the parametric feature-based modeling enables the automatic generation of fitted garments on differing body shapes. Consumers lean toward buying such apparel that are largely sold as designer apparel (Wang, Wang, and Yuen 2005).

Economics, Disruptive Dynamics, and Consumerism

Consumerism within the influence of socioeconomic factors becomes stronger as the consumer sovereignty is grown in the marketplace. Products targeted toward consumer segments derive their value solely from their contribution to the well-being of society and of individual consumers. Consumption activities are driven by the lifestyle goals and sustain if they satisfy the basic needs and provide social and personal distinctions in using the products and services. Consumers are also often interested in higher satisfaction by consuming innovative and socially differentiated products to achieve self-realization, fairness, freedom, participation, social relations, and balance among the consumption ecosystem. Such consumer aspirations may be served either by unique selling proposition, self-esteem, corporate image, or by new-generation products launched by the companies. For many consumers, consumption defines a significant part of their role in society, as sharing experience about products among peers helps in creating and maintaining relationships. It may be a basis for self-respect, and a significant part of what gives life interest and meaning. Consumerism has emerged historically across the changing market environment and has created mass markets, industrialization, and cultural attitudes that ensure that rising incomes are used to purchase an ever-growing output (Sharpe 2008).

In the highly competitive and global marketplace today, the pressure on organizations to find new ways to create and deliver value to customers grows even stronger. The global marketplace has been segmented geographically comprising triad market, pacific-rim, postcommunist countries, Latin America, China, and India. The Asian economies other than Japan have grown over 6 percent consistently during 2005 to 2006. Positive forces at work in retail consumer markets today include high rates of personal expenditures, low interest rates, low unemployment, and very low inflation. Negative factors that hold retail sales back involve weakening consumer confidence. In the last two decades, technological innovation, logistics, and supply chain have moved to the center stage. There has been a growing recognition that it is through an effective management of the logistics function and the supply chain that the goal of cost reduction and service enhancement can be achieved. The global marketplace may be described as a spatial network of markets across the countries comprising homogenous and customized segments. The emerging business models in the global marketplace include the following focus:

- Innovative products with economic advantages
- Developing consumerism with sociocultural differentiation
- Customer service orientation and satisfaction related to consumption
- Cocreation of products and services by involving consumers in the business process
- Customer value creation through experience sharing using social media
- Generating consumer-centric marketing environment for consumption of products and services, using digital marketing and business analytics to support decision making

The contemporary global business models explain that firms tend to structure themselves as one of the four organizational types: international, multidomestic, global, and transnational. Depending on the type, a company's assets and capabilities are either centralized or decentralized, knowledge is developed and diffused in either one direction or in many, and the importance of the overseas office to the home office varies. International marketing refers to exchanges across national boundaries for the satisfaction of human needs and wants. The various marketing functions coordinated and integrated across the multiple country markets may be referred as global marketing. The process of such integration may involve product standardization, uniform packaging, homogeneity in brand architecture, identical brand names, synchronized product positioning, and commonality in communication strategies or well-coordinated sales campaigns across the markets of different countries. The term "global" does not convey the literal meaning of penetration into all countries of the world. However, it needs to be understood in relative sense, and even a regionalization or operating in a cluster of countries may also be taken as a global operation in an applied perspective. The regional marketing efforts like trans-Asian or Pan-European marketing operations may also be viewed as examples of global marketing. The suppliers of products

ranging from Budweiser beer to BMW cars have been able to keep growing without succumbing to the pricing pressures and promotional environment. A strong brand can also open the door when growth depends
on breaking into new markets. Starbucks Corporation, among the
fastest-growing brands, recently set up shop in Vienna, one of Europe's
cafe capitals, among 400 new stores planned for opening at overseas locations. The companies succeed in the regional integration across multiple
country markets as they follow the similar strategies and management
principles for a cluster of markets. Consumerism in the global markets is
largely affected by the following corporate moves:

- Competitive differentiation of products and services
- Aggressive promotions, marketing communication, and
  advertisements
- Providing extensive consumer education and developing
  brand literacy
- Improving the longevity of product life and offering quality
  services
- Augmenting customer relations and delivering higher satisfac-
  tion to the consumers
- Developing convenience and leisure shopping models

The characteristics of the global marketplace are diverse, and international marketing approaches are different. Companies need to adopt
a strong rationale for grouping the countries into segments. The multinational and the global corporation are different as the former operates
in a number of countries and carries adjustment in the production and
marketing practices in each country at highly relative costs (Levitt 1998).
The global corporation operates with the stanch loyalty at relatively low
costs with standardization. Coca-Cola and Pepsi-Cola companies have
standardized their products globally according to the regional and ethnic
preferences of consumers. The most effective world competitors integrate
quality and trust attributes into their cost structure. Such companies
compete on the basis of appropriate value of price, quality, trust, and
delivery systems. The multinational corporations know a lot about the
business environment in a country, put their efforts on adapting to the

given environment, and set a gradual penetration process in the country. On the contrary, the global corporations recognize the absolute need to be competitive and drive through the lower prices by standardizing their marketing operations (Rajagopal 2008).

It is commonly assumed that the consumers' decision concerning the place they usually choose for shopping depends essentially on the distance to the mall. The satisfaction of shoppers plays an equally important role in metropolitan areas where there are numerous commercial zones to lead consumers to make decisions on shopping choices. Thus, different behavioral aspects including perception of shopping possibilities, expected pricing practices, and general global environment of each shopping mall affect the satisfaction or dissatisfaction of the consumers (Leo and Philippe 2002). Motivations of shopping include inside and outside ambiance of mall, layout, and extent of involvement in the shopping process. Ambiance of shopping mall, architecture, ergonomics, variety, and excitement motivate the shopper to stay long and make repeated visits to the mall. Common promotional activities employed by the stores in shopping malls include sales and encouragement to encourage the shoppers to make frequent visits to the mall. Some traditional promotions such as fashion shows and product displays are shown to be poor performer strategies in generating shopper's response, while mallwide sales are the preferred promotion. It is argued that a combination of general entertainment and price-oriented promotions are found to be strong alternatives to encourage customers to frequent visits and more spending (Parsons 2003). Hispanic shoppers including Mexican buyers make the trip to mall for shopping along with family and friends, and buy largely food and beverages during the visit. Hispanic shoppers also spend more time at the mall, shopping at various stores during their stay. Accordingly, marketers have become increasingly interested in the extent to which situational factors influence consumers' purchase behavior. An improved shopping ambiance and geo-demographic attraction of the marketplace largely help consumers in building their consumption behavior. In addition, companies make the following considerations in developing a consumer-friendly marketplace environment to create sustainable consumer perceptions to develop association with the brand and marketplace:

- Shopping mall attraction: assortment of stores, shopping space, leisure and information areas, accessibility, and parking
- Demonstrations, customer-centric retailing policies, and customer services
- Competitive advantage over product, price, place (availability), promotions, and people (sales)
- Ambiance of shopping mall in general and store in particular, economic sensitivity, ecological and environment friendly, and sharing peer experience

The three distinct dimensions of emotions, which include pleasantness, arousal, and mall attractiveness, have been identified as major drivers for making buying decisions among shoppers. The ambiance of shopping malls, whether pleasant or unpleasant, moderates the arousal effect on satisfaction, and in-store buying behaviors. Satisfaction in pleasant retail ambiance, where music, hands-on experience services, playing areas and recreation are integrated, maximizes the consumer arousal. It has been observed that young consumers perceive positive effect on in-store behaviors if shopping arousal is high. Thus, retailers need to pay attention not only to the pleasantness of the store environment, but also to arousal level expectations of shoppers (Wirtz, Mattila, and Tan 2007). The impact of inside mall ambiance can be measured in reference to the degree of stimulation and pleasure gained by consumers. Interactive tools on product learning provided in the retail stores significantly affect the level of arousal and pleasure, which contribute toward experience, and thereby influence the buying behavior. As higher stimulation or interactive learning provided by the retailers focuses on gaining initial experience on the product use, consumers tend to engage in higher arousing activities by acquiring the product (Menon and Kahn 2002).

The product attractiveness may comprise the product features like improved attributes, use of advance technology, innovativeness, extended product applications, brand augmentation, perceived use value, competitive advantages, corporate image, product advertisements, and sales and services policies associated therewith, which contribute in building sustainable customer values toward making buying decisions on the new products (Lafferty and Goldsmith 2004). The attractiveness of new products is one of the key factors affecting the decision making of customers and in turn is related to market growth and sales. The higher the positive reactions of the customers toward the new products in view of their attractiveness, higher the growth in sales.

Disruptive innovation may be described as the process that improves a product or service in a different way against the normal market drivers, typically first by developing a new consumer segment in a new market, or by defecting the consumers from the existing market. Most of the disruptive innovations are radical as they skip some stages of the process of the existing products and technologies to gain competitive advantages in the market quickly. In contrast to disruptive innovation, a sustaining innovation does not create new markets or value networks, but only evolves the existing ones with better value, allowing the firms to compete against each other's sustaining improvements. In view of the globalization and marketing practices of the emerging companies, it has been observed that market disruption has become a growth function for technology and its application.

Clayton M. Christensen has revolutionized the concept of disruptive innovation, which is referred as *technology mudslide hypothesis* (Christensen and Overdorf 2000). This is the simple notion expressing that an established firm fails because it is unable to cope up with the changing technological advances with the competing firms. In this hypothesis, attributes of a firm can be explained with the analogy of creepers—one that finds its own path to climb and the other that survives as a parasite to climb. Products emerging out of the disruptive technology are like parasites, which are built on the products available in the market with popular technologies. Disruptive innovation products largely focus on low cost and utilitarian values of the consumers. Good firms are usually aware of the emerging innovations underneath the market, but their business environment does not allow them to intersect the disruptive innovations as they are risky to pursue due to low profit and may drain resources of the firm. Generally, a firm's existing value networks place insufficient value on the disruptive innovation to allow its pursuit by another firm. Start-up firms live with different value networks until disruptive innovation is able to invade their value networks, grow parallel in the market and create a *me-too* entry, and strengthen its chances of cosurvival in the existing market.

Disruptive innovation may be a product or a service designed for a new set of customers by defecting them from the existing stream of buying. Generally, disruptive innovations are technologically straightforward, are convincing to consumers, and generate value for money. Some disruptive innovations offer more for less to customers through a different package of attributes that have higher significance to the consumers in the bottom-of-the-pyramid market segment than to those of the mainstream market. Major attributes of the disruptive innovations include:

- Low-price profile
- High perceived use value
- Low gross margins
- Small target markets
- Simple products and services
- Attractive solutions

Christensen argues that disruptive innovations can damage successful brands and well-managed products of reputed companies that are responsive to their customers, and have invested resources in conducting excellent research and development to support innovation. These companies tend to bypass markets that are most susceptible to disruptive innovations, as there is the risk of low profit and scope of business growth. Thus, disruptive technology provides products and services with focus on the customer, and drives strategically counterproductive impact on the existing products in a market. However, in a positive sense, the disruptive innovation may be considered as the constructive integration of attributes to the existing technology. Disruptive innovations generate radical insights that could help in improving the economic benefits to consumers, and provide better opportunities for the firms to grow in mass market.

The low-end disruptive innovation products are targeted to customers, who are satisfied even with the partial performance of the product but derive high emotional satisfaction. On the other hand, new-market disruption aims at the new consumer segment to cater both high product performance as well as emotional satisfaction. Low-end disruption in market takes place when the demand for the product exists but products are unavailable. Consumers have the latent desire to experience the high-end products, but often these products are not affordable. Consequently, at some point, the performance of the disruptive products overshoots the needs of certain customer segments and, at this point, a disruptive technology may enter the market and provide a product with high-perceived use value, gaining a reasonable market share. In low-end disruption, the disruptive product is focused initially on serving the least profitable customer, who is happy with the partial performance of the product. Such customers will be willing to pay lower price than others and have higher satisfaction on having the product over its performance. Once the disruptive products gain a sustainable market share, it seeks to improve its profit margin over the established brands. And to achieve higher profit margins, the disruptive products enter the differentiated price segment, where the customer is willing to pay a little more for higher quality. Hence, the disruptor firms set the innovation process for the products to meet the desired quality and establish as a back-market product. Over time the disruptive products will move to up-market, and focus on penetrating into attractive consumer segments. This business situation makes the disruptive products to spur out of the niche. The new market disruption occurs when a product fits a new or emerging market segment that is not being served by existing incumbents in the industry (Rajagopal 2014).

Summary

The competition in the marketplace today is growing manifold, offering consumers a wide range of options for making buying decisions. Consumer behavior is therefore a dynamic process, involving random shifts in the consumption culture as well. Consumer products companies are engaged in creating differentiated products and services for their consumers to attract them toward new experiences and evaluate the competitive advantages. Consumers learn about new options from advertising, and many consumers develop variety-seeking behavior over time. Though consumer cultures vary across the markets and geo-demographic segments, the social interactions on the digital space, peer networking, and consumer communities often moderate the consumer behavior in a competitive marketplace. Consumer behavior is also altered often by the disruptive innovations and associated market economies. This chapter discusses the overall scenario on globalization and its effects on the consumer behavior. However, it is difficult to draw conclusion on changing behavioral perspectives of consumers as they are psychologically complicated. Optimistically, this chapter argues that, despite the transition in consumer behavior, companies explore opportunities to improve their performance in existing markets and break into new markets.

References

Almquist, E., J. Senior, and N. Bloch. 2016. "Elements of Value." *Harvard Business Review* 94, no. 9, pp. 46–53.

Bianchi, M. 2002. "Novelty, Preferences, and Fashion: When Goods are Unsettling." *Journal of Economic Behavior & Organization* 47, 1, pp. 1–18.

Bhattacharya, A.K., and D.C. Michael. 2008. "How Local Companies Keep Multinationals at Bay." *Harvard Business Review* 86, no. 3, pp. 84–95.

Bremmer, I. 2014. "The New Rules of Globalization." *Harvard Business Review* 92, no. 1, pp. 103–7.

Brucks, M., V.A. Zeithaml, and G. Naylor. 2000. "Price and Brand Name as Indicators of Quality Dimensions of Customer Durables." *Journal of Academy of Marketing Science* 28, no. 3, pp. 359–74.

Cleveland, M., and M. Laroche. 2007. "Acculturation to the Global Consumer Culture: Scale Development and Research Paradigm." *Journal of Business Research* 60, no. 3, pp. 249–59.

Christensen, C.M., and M. Overdorf. 2000. "Meeting the Challenge of Disruptive Change." *Harvard Business Review* 78, no. 2, pp. 66–76.

Davenport, T.H. 2009. "How to Design Smart Business Experiments." *Harvard Business Review* 87, no. 2, pp. 68–76.

Davies, A. October 2004. "Moving Base into High-Value Integrated Solutions: A Value Stream Approach." *Industrial and Corporate Change* 13, no. 5, pp. 727–56.

Donkers, B., P.C. Verhoef, and D.J. Martijn. April 2003. *Predicting Customer Lifetime Value in Multi-Service Industries*, ERIM Report Series.

Eisenhardt, K.M., and S.L. Brown. 1998. "Time Pacing: Competing in Markets That Won't Stand Still." *Harvard Business Review* 76, no. 2, pp. 59–69.

Hartley, J., and L. Montgomery. 2009. "Fashion as Consumer Entrepreneurship: Emergent Risk Culture, Social Network Markets, and the Launch of Vogue in China." *Chinese Journal of Communication* 2, no. 1, pp. 61–76.

Hedaa, L., and T. Ritter. 2005. "Business Relationships on Different Waves: Paradigm Shift and Marketing Orientation Revisited." *Industrial Marketing Management* 34, no. 7, pp. 714–21.

Hensmans, M. 2017. "Competing Through Joint Innovation." *MIT Sloan Management Review* 58, no. 2, pp. 26–34.

Horowitz, D.M. 2009. "A Review of Consensus Analysis Methods in Consumer Culture, Organizational Culture and National Culture Research." *Consumption Markets & Culture* 12, no. 1, pp. 47–64.

Jansson, J., and D. Power. 2010. "Fashioning a Global City: Global City Brand Channels in the Fashion and Design Industries." *Regional Studies* 44, no. 7, pp. 889–904.

Kerr, W.R. 2016. "Harnessing the Best of Globalization." *MIT Sloan Management Review* 58, no. 1, pp. 59–67.

Kim, C.W., and R.A. Mauborgne. 1999. "Creating New Market Space." *Harvard Business Review* 77, no. 1, pp. 3–93.

Kumar, N. 2006. "Strategies to Fight Low-Cost Rivals." *Harvard Business Review* 84, no. 12, pp. 104–12.

Lafferty, B.A., and R.E. Goldsmith. 2004. "How Influential is Corporate Credibility and Endorser Attractiveness When Innovators React to Advertisement for a New High Technology Product?" *Corporate Reputation Review* 7, no. 1, pp. 24–6.

Leo, P.Y., and J. Philippe. 2002. "Retail Centers: Location and Consumer's Satisfaction." *The Service Industries Journal* 22, no. 1, pp. 122–46.

Liu, T.C., and L.W. Wu. 2007. "Customer Retention and Cross-Buying in the Banking Industry: An Integration of Service Attributes, Satisfaction and Trust." *Journal of Financial Services Marketing* 12, no. 2, pp. 132–45.

Martin-Herran, G., S.P. Sigue, and G. Zaccour. 2010. "The Dilemma of Pull and Push-Price Promotions." *Journal of Retailing* 86, no. 1, pp. 51–68.

Menon, S., and B. Kahn. 2002. "Cross-Category Effects of Induced Arousal and Pleasure on the Internet Shopping Experience." *Journal of Retailing* 78, no. 1, pp. 31–40.

Moon, J., D. Chadee, and S. Tikoo. 2008. "Culture, Product Type, and Price Influences on Consumer Purchase Intention to Buy Personalized Products Online." *Journal of Business Research* 61, no. 1, pp. 31–9.

Parsons, A.G. 2003. "Assessing the Effectiveness of Shopping Mall Promotions: Customer Analysis." *International Journal of Retail & Distribution Management* 31, no. 2, pp. 74–9.

Pinheiro, M. 2008. "Loyalty, Peer Group Effects, and 401(k)." *The Quarterly Review of Economics and Finance* 48, no. 1, pp. 94–122.

Piron, F. 2006. "China's Changing Culture: Rural and Urban Consumers' Favorite Things." *Journal of Consumer Marketing* 23, no. 6, pp. 327–34.

Rajagopal., and R. Sanchez. 2004. "Conceptual Analysis of Brand Architecture and Relations within Product Categories." *The Journal of Brand Management* 11, no. 3, pp. 233–47.

Rajagopal 2008. "Measuring Brand Performance through Metrics Application." *Measuring Business Excellence* 12, no. 1, pp. 29–38.

Rajagopal 2009. "Effects of Customer Services Efficiency and Market Effectiveness on Dealer Performance." *International Journal of Services and Operations Management* 5, no. 5, pp. 575–94.

Rajagopal 2011. "Consumer Culture and Purchase Intentions towards Fashion Apparel in Mexico." *Journal of Database Marketing and Consumer Strategy Management* 18, no. 4, pp. 286–307.

Rajagopal 2012. "Brand Manifestation and Retrieval Effects as Drivers of Buying Behavior in Mexico." *Journal of Database Marketing and Consumer Strategy Management* 19, no. 3, pp. 179–96.

Rajagopal 2014. *Architecting Enterprise: Managing Innovation, Technology, and Global Competitiveness.* Basingstoke, Hampshire, UK: Palgrave Macmillan.

Roberto, M.A., and C.L. Lynne. 2005. "Art of Making Change Initiative Sticks." *Sloan Management Review* 46, no. 4, pp. 53–60.

Rucker, D.D., and A.D. Galinsky. 2009. "Conspicuous Consumption Versus Utilitarian Ideals: How Different Levels of Power Shape Consumer Behavior." *Journal of Experimental Social Psychology* 45, no. 3, pp. 549–55.

Sankaran, K., and C. Demangeot. 2011. "On Becoming a Culturally Plural Consumer." *Journal of Consumer Marketing* 28, no. 7, pp. 540–49.

Seo, Y., and K.S. Fam. 2015. "Researching Asian Consumer Culture in the Global Marketplace." *Qualitative Market Research: An International Journal* 18, no. 4, pp. 386–90.

Seock, Y.K., and L.R. Bailey. 2009. "Fashion Promotions in the Hispanic Market: Hispanic Consumers' Use of Information Sources in Apparel Shopping." *International Journal of Retail & Distribution Management* 37, no. 2, pp. 161–81.

Sharpe, M.E. 2008. *Microeconomics in Context.* Philadelphia, PA: Routledge.

Smedslund, J. 2011. "Meaning of Words and the Use of Axiomatics in Psychological Theory." *Journal of Theoretical & Philosophical Psychology* 31, no. 2, pp. 126–35.

Svensson, G. 2002. "Beyond Global Marketing and the Globalization of Marketing Activities." *Management Decision* 40, no. 6, pp. 574–83.

Tallman. S., and K. Fladmoe-Lindquist. 2002. "Internationalization, Globalization, and Capability-Based Strategy." *California Management Review* 45, no. 1, pp. 116–35.

Venkatesh, A., A. Joy, J.F. Sherry, and J. Deschenes. 2010. "The Aesthetics of Luxury Fashion, Body and Identify Formation." *Journal of Consumer Psychology* 20, no. 4, pp. 459–70.

Villanueva, J., P. Bharadwaj, Y. Chen, and S. Balasubramanian. May 2004. *Managing Customer Relationships-Should Managers Really Focus on Long Term*, IESE Business School, Working Paper # D/560, pp. 1–37.

Voss, M.D., R.J. Calantone, and S.B. Keller. 2005. "Internal Service Quality: Determinants of Distribution Center Performance." *International Journal of Physical Distribution & Logistics Management* 35, no. 3, pp. 161–76.

Wakefield, K.L., and J.J. Inman. 2003. "Situational Price Sensitivity: The Role of Consumption Occasion, Social Context and Income." *Journal of Retailing* 79, no. 4, pp. 199–212.

Wang, C.C.L., Y. Wang, and M.M.F. Yuen. 2005. "Design Automation for Customized Apparel Products." *Computer-Aided Design* 37, no. 7, pp. 675–91.

Wirtz, J., A.S. Mattila, and R.L.P. Tan. 2007. "The Role of Arousal Congruency in Influencing Consumers' Satisfaction Evaluations and in-Store Behaviors." *International Journal of Service Industry Management* 18, no. 1, pp. 6–24.

CHAPTER 2

Consumer Impetus and Business Management

Overview

Consumer behavior is complex, and companies have a major challenge to understand the behavioral intricacies from managerial points of view. Several behavioral theories emerged in the past explaining the cognitive perspectives of consumers, which also guide the managers to develop appropriate marketing strategies. This chapter discusses consumer motivational, cognitive and physical, and consumer acquisition- and retention-related theories. Among others the acquiescence effect, acquired needs theory, activation theory, affect infusion model, decision appraisal theory, attribution theory, Cannon–Bard theory of emotions, consistency theory, choice theory, cognitive appraisal theory, and conversion theory have been discussed in this chapter in the context of business impetus of companies. This chapter also discusses the new routes to market for consumers and their implications on the business.

Understanding Consumer Behavior

Business in 21st century has turned consumer centric, and marketing strategies are knitted around consumers. Consumer behavior is complex and often unpredictable. It is driven by social, cultural, personal, and economic needs of consumers. Most companies, which tend to engage consumers in gaining knowledge about brands, values, corporate image, and competitive advantage, use proactive consumer strategies. Higher involvement of consumers in brands delivers comprehensive experience and inculcates perceived use value. Understanding consumer behavior is crucial for effective marketing, designing attractive deliverables, and generating awareness about the brands. Due to the growing competition in the markets, globalization, and changing sociocultural trends among the consumers, it has become essential to understand various perceptions of consumers in developing an appropriate marketing plan.

Consumer behavior is largely driven by the needs and the available solutions to meet the demands of consumers. Instead of merely buying products and services, consumers today look for solutions to their existing and potential problems. Accordingly, in the competitive market environment today, consumers tend to experiment more solutions and develop their perceptions on the best-fit matches. Consumer perceptions are sensitive to their experiences, and help in building attitude if sustained for a reasonable period. Most consumer-centric companies ensure that consumers gain favorable and sustainable perception, through branding campaigns, digital communications, social media forums, and product and services trials. The trials are designed to deliver brand knowledge, product attributes, peer experience, social and personal values, and competitive advantage, to strengthen the consumer perceptions. A perception on the product or services is an instant feeling for the consumer that could create impression about it at the first trial. Successful marketing campaigns not only bring awareness to a product, but also establish its place somewhere on the hierarchy of needs.

To build sustainable perceptions of consumers on products and services brands, companies maintain consistency on brand communication, attributes of products, quality, and prescribed use value. Often companies tag the best prescription to the product, and build brand promise accordingly. For example, BMW has the brand tag as "ultimate driving machine," while Apple Inc. embeds the brand tag to its innovative technology products as "think different." Once such brand tags raise sustainable consumer perception through brand experience and peer values, the cognitive drivers to the perception turn sustainable and appear as consumer attitude. This situation not only positions the product or brand as "top-of-the-mind" element, but also drives continuity of its usage among the consumers. Such attitude reflects in the repeat buying behavior, and sharing of brand experience extensively over the interpersonal and digital platforms, by the consumers. As the consumer attitude stays sustainable across the spatial and temporal dimensions in the marketplace, it turns as consumer behavior, which is hard to change.

Companies motivate consumers to prioritize their choice and purchase intentions within the hierarchical needs of consumers. High value-led perception among consumers on the products and services instills a sense of need confidence and urgency in their behavior. Marketers have been able to use motivational and need-based strategies effectively, by creating endorsing perceptions and attitudes on brands among consumers. The needs include, in order of importance, physiological (survival), safety, love, esteem, and self-actualization. Business schools and marketing classes adapted Maslow's theories to explain the need to tailor marketing messages to consumers in an appealing way. Modern luxury carmakers highlighting the safety and security features of their vehicles over the esthetic value create emotional perceptions. Consumers perceive safety as primary need for using an automobile, and consider it as value for money. Sharing experience on perceptions and attitude, consumers influence other consumers as well. The experiential marketing helps companies to socialize brands and gain competitive advantage in the marketplace. Ethnocentrism also provides marketers with the information necessary to target consumers such as cultural, religious, or nationalistic feelings to influence perceptions of consumers and purchase behavior.

Perceptions of consumers on products, services, and brands are largely affected by varied ecosystems built around the personal and social attributes. Personal attributes that commonly influence consumer perceptions include value for money, quality, comfort, brand reputation, innovation, technology, use value, and competitive advantages. The affinity of consumers for a product or service depends on the various types of affinity marketing programs, including sponsorship of social causes, sports, or entertainment events. In competitive marketplace, consumers compare brand attributes to gain new insights to develop cross-brand perceptions and lean toward most appropriate purchase intentions by distinguishing brand attributes and consumer preferences. Consumers also develop perceptions on brands considering their affiliations with social causes like sports, corporate responsibility, public concerns, destination images, or entertainment events. In emerging markets, brands supported by social cause campaigns often receive grater attractions than regular brand communications. YUWA, a nonprofit organization that teaches girls to play football to overcome the challenges in their life, has been showcased by Lenovo Inc. This campaign of the Lenovo computer company portrayed the young girls who represented India at Donosti Cup in Spain in 2016. Lenovo India, in association with YUWA, invested in a massive cause marketing campaign, "Girls with Goals." The idea was to highlight their journey in real time, as the girls made their way from the hinterland of Jharkhand state in India to Spain. Lenovo could drive several consumers into its manifold corporate social responsibility focus and succeeded in bringing its brand to the top-of-the mind perception of consumers.

Consumer perceptions are often fragile and complex as well. Their value streams on brands, products, and services are asymmetric and uncertain as they are more influenced by the peers and society than self-perceptions. Hence, perceptions turn uncertain, and consumers find it difficult to develop purchase intentions and take buying decisions. Self-perception theory explains that individuals develop an understanding of the motivations behind their own behavior. Self-perception by customers relates to values and motivations that drive buying behavior. Consumers' self-perception drives their intentions and decisions on whether to get associated with the conscious purchase and consumption practices. Most consumers view themselves as socially conscious as they hold right perceptions of brands, products, and services, and tend to place more weight on self-derived values while making buying decisions. Perceptions take long time to develop into an attitude. However, building attitude in marketplace is often impulsive for consumers than judgmental as attitude is largely determined by the pressure of consumer needs, available choices, and sustainable consumer perceptions. Impulsive attitudes emerge out of consumer psychodynamics and peer pressure due to some obsessive attributes of the brands, products, or services like low price and sales promotion offers raised by the companies.

In the early 21st century, air travel has become necessary for a large number of consumers due to rapid growth of business and working avenues, and time and resources constraints. Such consumer need has prompted market competition in aviation sector and attracted many low-cost airline companies posing threat to long-standing and sustainable airline companies. The low-cost airlines adapted the policy of lowering the price of tickets per trip by curtailing the inflight and ground services amenities. The low-price promotions gave a big boom to the market share of low-cost airlines, but consumers were critical about reducing the services and charging additional fee for inflight food and beverages.

There have been mixed perceptions among consumers in adapting to the low-cost airline brands, and it took over a decade of 2001 to create an explicit attitude among consumers compromising the weaknesses in services. However, as more airlines have adopted similar policies, consumer choices of airlines were narrowed down, while the need for air travel increased. Hence, the consumer perceptions were compromised at the cost of growing work pressures and frequency of travel that turned the altered quality of services as an attitude. The examples may be cited of Spirit Airlines (the United States), Southwest Airlines (the United States), Ryan Air (Ireland), and Indigo Airlines (India) that emerged as potential low-cost airlines and successfully altered the consumer behavior and attitude toward the air travel.

Consumer perception is also derived by the sensory perceptions to marketing and advertising tactics. Sensory perception relates to the way consumers perceive and process sensory stimuli on the brand, and critically appraise opinions of fellow consumers about companies and the merchandise. Most companies apply consumer perception theory to determine how their customers perceive their brands, products, and services. They also use consumer perception theory to develop marketing and advertising strategies intended to retain current customers and attract new ones. Perception, attitude, and behavior of consumers is a linear process that helps companies understand and define the decision process of consumers. This cognitive chain retains the product information in memory, and analyzes with reference to its value dimensions over the period. Among many, the simplest cognitive level that derives perceptions of consumers on products is the satisfaction gained through the product, while the most complex perceptual dimension is the value for money, or payoff of the product to the consumer. Young and Barbara (1975) depicted this view in the *grey benefit chain*, which illustrates how a product is linked through a chain of benefits to a concept called the emotional payoff. The means-end chain approach to understanding the cognitive structure of consumers holds that product information is retained in memory at several levels of abstraction. Aggregate cognitive mapping, structural analysis, cognitive differentiation analysis, and value structure mapping are techniques designed especially to analyze and represent higher-order abstractions such as quality. These techniques are more appropriate than preference mapping or multiattribute modeling for investigating concepts like quality and value (Zeithaml 1988).

Consumer Motivational Theories

Consumers are motivated by various sources and strategies of the companies. Competitive advantages and product differentiations on products and services communicated by the companies to the consumers, social and peer influence, and consumer-generated contents are the most effective sources of consumers to get motivated and make purchase decisions. A company in a business market, therefore, manages customers individually, showing how its products or services can help solve each buyer's problems, and benefit them comparatively to others. Chinese consumers remain motivated, brand conscious, and focus on perceived value and derived satisfaction so intensely that brand loyalty is often secondary. The needs or interests of their families have greater importance for them than materialistic values of the products and services. Word of mouth has become a significant channel of product information and an instant motivating source. Attracting and motivating consumers to the stores will always be at the top of the mind of companies. In the future, making the shopping experience more a form of family entertainment could prove fruitful, for example, putting restaurants on the premises of stores, adding children's play areas, or opening adjacent movie complexes.

Acquiescence Effect

There are many motivational theories that still guide managers to attract consumers, retain them over the changing preferences, and develop loyalty. One of the most vulnerable cognitive dimensions among the consumers is acquiescence effect, which has several implications in the decision analytics of a consumer. This effect inculcates a sense of superiority and exhibitionism among consumers by evaluating self over others, as "how a consumer will appear to others?" Another person can explain such cognitive dimension upon asking a question about how he or she looks. From the consumers' point of view, they consider such state of mind as superiority complex. Most consumer-oriented companies trigger such psychodynamics among the consumers by launching advertising campaigns that are informative as well as challenging. Nissan Automobile had brought to the market "Shift the future" campaign in 2002, with an intention to draw the acquiescence effect among the mass consumers. Consumers observe the acquiescence effect to the needs against others, particularly when:

- They seem to be a superior in some way;
- They have a need whereby we can easily help them;
- Responding to other consumers or in the social media will really become hard.

Often acquiescence effect among consumers is turned as forced choice. Generally, companies present comparative benefits to the consumers to create such effect. For instance, Unilever had launched a commercial for its detergent cake in India with the verbal conversation "Mine is whiter than yours" in 2006. This commercial has been successful in attracting consumers and creating stronger acquiescence effect among consumers.

Acquiescence bias is a cognitive state, in which consumer tends to agree with all propositions or positive connotation that a communication of a company delivers. Acquiescence effect may also be explained as "yea-saying" or the friendliness bias, which occurs when a consumer demonstrates a tendency to agree with the given situation, and be positive with the product or service delivered or communicated. In other words, they think every idea is a good idea, and can see themselves liking, buying, and acting upon every option that is proposed. Some consumers have acquiescent personalities, while others acquiesce because they perceive others are better than they are. Creating the acquiescence effect among consumers is the easy way out for companies, as it takes less effort than carefully weighing each option and ensures quick strategy for driving motivation.

Acquired Needs Theory

David McClelland proposed that an individual's specific needs are acquired and shaped by his experiences over time. Most of these needs can be categorized as achievement, affiliation, and power. A person's motivation and effectiveness in certain decisions on consumption are influenced by the aforementioned taxonomy. Cognitively a consumer describes his achievement over the need in terms of the degree of satisfaction gained in reference to his decision on buying. The decision on new products and services embedded with innovation and technology often becomes complex for the consumers, as it is difficult to measure the level of achievement or satisfaction emerging on their decision. Consumers set goals, strive to take moderate risks, challenging but aiming to achieve sustainable satisfaction, prefer unique and solo experimentation, and set their perceived values on using the products and services. The motive behind need for achievement is commonly to improve the previous values and quality of experience. Consumers' need for achievement triggers in reference to food, shelter, clothing, health care, job security, safety, income security, and other levels within Maslow's hierarchy of needs (McClelland 1978). The applied dimensions of acquired needs theory from the point of view of companies engaged in managing consumers are exhibited in Figure 2.1.

Decision conformity is the core attribute, which influences the acquired needs perspectives of consumers established through the three prime determinants comprising consumer achievement, affiliation, and consumer power, as exhibited in Figure 2.1. Consumer-centric companies should understand the cognitive evolution among consumers, and develop strategies for corporate push accordingly. The determinant of consumer achievement cognitively evolves among consumers in a sequential path from identifying felt needs over the acquired needs. Consumers tend to

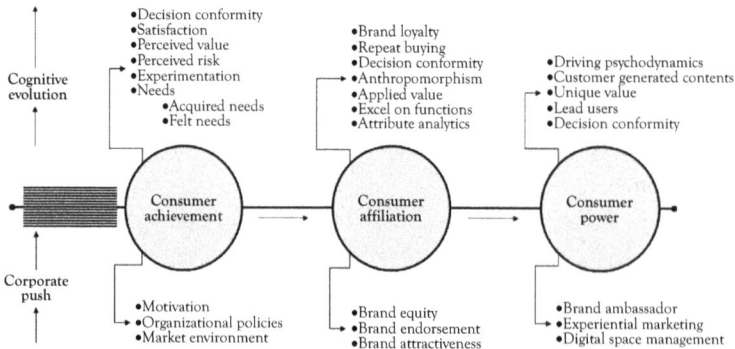

Figure 2.1 Acquired needs theory: Applied dimensions

experiment relevant brands and analyze perceived risk over the perceived value to measure desired satisfaction. During such cognitive process consumers gradually reach to their decision whether to associate with the brand or otherwise. To support the cognitive evolution among consumers in achieving satisfaction, companies should improve their organizational policies in view of competitive marketplace, and develop motivational approaches accordingly. Consumers who achieve satisfaction by using products and services for the identified needs, and justify their decision, further move to the stage of affiliation with the company and the brand. This stage is highly significant to the companies, as consumers get engaged in analyzing the attributes of products and services, excel on their functions, evaluate perceived use value, measure anthropomorphic value, find conformity to the decision, and indulge in repeat buying. And if all the stages in the affiliation process are successful, most consumers develop the attitude of brand loyalty. Companies need to improve brand attractiveness and promote brands through celebrity endorsement, so that consumers can personify the brands, and get affiliated to the brands and the company. A strong affiliation to the brands inculcates the power of leadership among consumers as illustrated in Figure 2.1. Most consumers, turned lead users, feel empowered with their decision, and take the lead to guide the other consumers (early adopters, early majority, and late majority) toward the brands, products, and services. Upon analyzing the variables of first two determinants, achievement and affiliation, consumers reach to the final determinant of consumer power, wherein they react with the marketplace in general, and peers in particular, by posting customer-generated contents on the digital space. This is a delicate stage for companies, who should meticulously manage their digital space for communication, engage in experiential marketing, and promote brand ambassadors among the consumers to empower their cognitive strength.

Consumers with a high need for achievement seek to excel on the functions of products and services, and tend to avoid both low-risk and high-risk situations. Consumers avoid low-risk situations, so that they can quickly achieve satisfaction. In high-risk buying decisions, consumers take chance to achieve satisfaction, and prefer to get associated with such decision critically moderating the probability of success. On theoretical grounds, there is no reason why a person, who has a strong need to be more efficient, should be a successful consumer. While it sounds as if everyone identifies the need to achieve, streamlining the motivation and achievement leads consumers to experiment with the new products and services, and drives their decision to influence early adopters, early majority, and late majority consumer categories. The need for affiliation among consumers is a conscious drive in view of the AATAR factors comprising awareness, attributes, trial, availability, and repeat buying. The success of trial of products among consumers congruent to their decision leads to repeat buying, which creates affiliation or belongingness of consumers to the brand (Rajagopal 2010a).

Consumers who succeed in getting high satisfaction mark their decision as an achievement and seek affiliation with the brand or product. These consumers look for developing harmonious relationships with other people and look for other people to accept their decision, style, or the way of using the product to achieve high satisfaction. Consumers tend to conform to the norms of social needs by widening their brand affiliation and product usage. Consumers feel empowered when their decisions are right. They seek and obtain leadership positions in social groups, professional associations, and with the sales people (Uduji and Ankeli 2013). Consumers with different needs are motivated differently. The need can be fulfilled through social, friendships, and acceptance programs that would empower the consumers.

Activation Theory: Motivational Push

Consumers often need a motivational push to activate their need and action toward implementing the decision. Consumer-centric companies often launch advertising and communication campaigns to drive consumers by using several motivational tactics in reference to price, promotion, customer services, product and services delivery and guarantee, and technology benefits. The uniqueness of products and services, and scope of consumer stand-alone in the marketplace, develops the "me too" feeling and generates arousal among consumers to experiment products, develops intention to purchase, and develops perceived value. Arousal is a variable directly related to cognitive and affective processes, which orients consumer mind to react to external stimuli. In broad sense, arousal is a physiological and psychological state of alertness (Belanche, Flavián, and Pérez-Rueda 2014). As a fundamental dimension in the study of emotions, arousal has been related to simple processes such as awareness and attention, and more complex tasks such as information retention and attitude formation. Arousal is one of the strongest cognitive responses to motivation.

Activation theory describes how cognitive arousal is necessary for effective functioning of people and achieving desired satisfaction. A person requires a certain level of activation psychologically, physiologically, and environmentally in order to get sufficiently motivated to achieve goals, take right decisions, follow logical action, and get perfect convergence with motivations, mind, and means. Consumers seek activation to justify needs, refine preferences, make right decisions, develop perceived value, and get associated with the products or services. Companies tend to motivate consumers through advertising and communication to educate them, help them gain experience through "do-it-yourself" virtual and physical platforms, online simulations, and share experience on digital media. However, in this process consumers are also explained about the novelty, complexity, variations, and uncertainty in delivering the prescribed value of products and services. Motivational push is strategically planned and delivered by the consumer-centric companies to increase awareness, developing sense of ownership (*me too* feeling), and ways to inculcate value on the products and services.

Affect Infusion Model

Consumer moods, eventuality, perseverance, and aggression are the principal constituents of the affect infusion model. This model attempts to explain how mood affects one's ability to process information. A key assertion of the paradigm is that the effects of mood tend to be aggravated in complex situations that demand substantial cognitive processing. As situations become more complicated and unanticipated for a person to manage, mood becomes more influential in driving evaluation process and objective responses. Cognitively, mood of a person often affects the decision-making process and judgment. Several factors related to the consumer judgment, needs, target, context, and external influence play role in moderating the decision process. Accordingly, this model indicates that mood and emotion exert a notable influence not only on information processing, but also on the resulting response behaviors. Since mood and emotions play a greater role in consumer decision, most consumer products and services companies develop familiarity of consumers with the target group to motivate consumers. However, if a target is complex or unusual, it is more likely to trigger substantive processing. Otherwise, heuristic processing is generally used to motivate the consumers. The affect infusion model argues that the positive effect is more closely linked to heuristic processing, while negative effect is more closely associated with substantive processing of decision and judgmental reasoning.

Consumers often develop ambiguity in preferences, judgments, and value perceptions. Thus, making a right decision among identical and similar brands raises disputed cognitive boundaries among consumers. The ambiguity effect is a cognitive bias where decision making is affected by lack of information. In context of consumers, such effect is caused due to the unclear brand communications delivered by the companies through the advertisements and campaigns, and digital information that goes viral without appropriate checks. The effect implies that consumers tend to select options for which the probability of a favorable outcome is known and tested by others.

Cognitive and Physical Convergence Theories

Consumer attitudes developed over the long-sustained perception, and actual behaviors, are commonly aligned unless the attitudes over time have shown cognitive disruption (abrupt shifts in attitude). Consumers have many opportunities to express attitude through behavior. However, sometimes attitude and behavior are both constrained to very specific circumstances. Consumer attitudes are based on personal experience, and are endorsed by either the previous self-experience or peers. Attitude is strongly built around core beliefs of consumers on temporal, spatial, and personal experiences.

Attitude-behavior consistency among consumers exists, when there is a strong relation between consumer perceptions, purchase intentions, actions, and perceived value. For example, a consumer with an attitude of buying green products exhibits concern about the environment, and recycling paper and bottles. The sustainability in attitude develops behavioral consistency over time among consumers. Companies need to develop strategies to encourage such attitude-behavior consistency among consumers, as it is important for cocreating behavior among potential consumers and guiding their actions (Verma and Duggal 2015). To develop attitude-behavior consistency, consumer products companies should meticulously understand the consumer ecosystem, which is formed with various social, cultural, and personal attributes. The market communication and scope of products or services need to fit into the consumer ecosystem, which would help consumers to develop perceptions and values. Consumer ecosystem that affects the cognitive decision process by developing perception-attitude-behavior process is exhibited in Figure 2.2.

Consumer ecosystem is constituted broadly by the four powers comprising corporate, sociocultural, personal, and ambiance attributes, as illustrated in Figure 2.2, that help consumer toward developing attribute-behavior consistency. The corporate attributes of consumer products companies include brand communications specifying product attributes, which are divulged through advertisements and promotions of products and services. Most companies disseminate consumer experience via digital networks, and social media platforms, and encourage exchange of word of mouth through conventional modes. The corporate attributes significantly influence the consumer perceptions and help in building

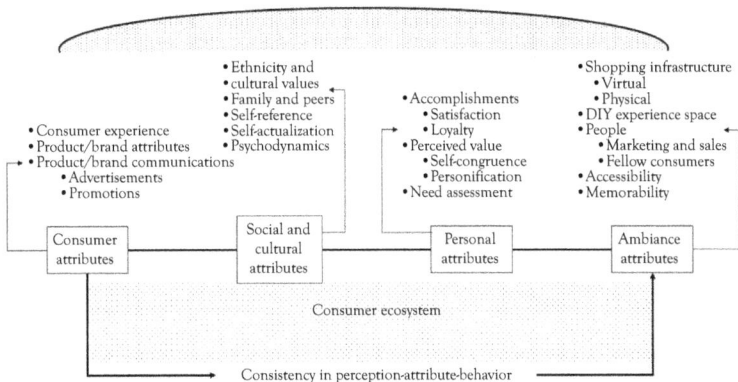

Figure 2.2 Consumer ecosystem for cognitive decision process

attitude and behavior through stronger beliefs, self-reference, and confidence on the values of products and services, and corporate image as well. The social and cultural attributes that influence consumer ecosystem in moderating the cognitive decision process encompass ethnicity and cultural values, effects of family and peers, self-reference showing confidence in the decision process, self-congruence upon finding the perfect match of decisions with the actual behavior leading to satisfaction, and psychodynamics—driving through the interpersonal word of mouth and digital space. Ethnicity abides the consumers within their cultural ambiance and brings them closer to their lifestyle. Consumers feel easier and safer to adapt to such an ecosystem and develop favorable perceptions on the products or services, and consistency in their attitude and behavior over time.

Consumer perceptions are largely governed by personal attributes like determining right needs and finding a right match of products or services to maximize perceived value (satisfaction) as exhibited in Figure 2.2. Anthropomorphism is another significant attribute that delivers high perceived value, and inculcates the sense of association with brands and the feeling of belongingness with the company. Most consumer-centric companies use anthropomorphic measures through brand engrossment communications, like *I am Telcel* (a telecommunication company in Mexico) and *I am Totally Palacio* (Palacio de Hierro is a departmental chain store in Mexico), and anthropomorphic characters in Walt Disney movies, *Ratatouille*. The controlling factor of the brand's anthropomorphism is based on the customers' lifestyles. A Harley Davidson biker is on the road all the time in packs and groups, who is looking to explore with a need for strong masculine perception. The bike in the advertisement shoves on the road and roars for freedom, independence, and unity with other users. Such brand communications deliver anthropomorphic effects on consumer perceptions, and augment the perceived use value leading to satisfaction and loyalty. In addition, attributes concerning the shopping ambiance in reference to retail infrastructure (virtual and physical), *do-it-yourself* space for product experience, sales people and fellow consumers, routes to market to access products or services, and memorability of consumer experience also build the ecosystem to drive the cognitive decision process among consumers.

Decision Appraisal Theory

In order to build live brands, companies develop features or identifiable metaphors, which give a personified feel of a brand, enabling connection and communication with the consumers. A brand's verbal elements poetically comprise demonstrating characters, stories, personality, imagery, music, and other representative components, to deliver anthropomorphic effect among consumers in developing sustainable perceptions and consistency in the attitude-behavior process among consumers. Most consumer-centric companies communicate brands through advertisements and peer interactivity in a way that builds emotions among consumers and helps in developing perceptions over time. Emotions play a significant role in developing right perceptions and making decisions among consumers. Emotions are extracted from situational evaluations, appraisals of communication, and trial of products or services that raise specific observations among consumers. Essentially, appraisal of a situation causes an emotional or affective response among consumers, which stands as a base for further judgments on adaptability of products or services, quality of the brand, and building perceived value. In a competitive marketplace, new brands emerge continuously, existing brands are renovated, and disruptive brands appear as well. Consumers appraise them, assess them against various criteria, and try them to develop perceived values. Emotions emerge during this process and guide consumers in making decisions for the long-term association with the brand or company.

Consumers appraise several brands and products in real time, and analyze their perceptions and associated emotions categorically. Consumers also stay reflective, brainstorming, and analytical about their experience with the brands and products, and feel good or bad about them accordingly. Emotions are valence and specific affective reactions to the perception of situations, events, objects, or people. They influence thoughts, motivations, and behaviors, and can play an important role in family business strategy and decision making. Specific discrete emotions influence judgments and decision-making processes (Bee and Neubaum 2014). A structural model of appraisal describes the relationships among perceptions, appraisal, and mediation the consumers use in making decisions. The attributes of these elements are discussed as follows:

Perception: advertising, reviews, public relations, social media, personal experiences, and other channels about the brand attributes and performance typically govern a consumer's perception.

Appraisal: appraisal of a consumer is the process, which evaluates the perceived attributes of the brand in terms of values on a set of measures and judgmental dimensions.

Mediation: this process relates appraisal values to the emotions of consumers. The mediation helps consumers to bridge the hidden gaps in their observations and emotions, while appraising a brand in a supermarket, retail store, or marketplace in general.

Primarily consumers appraise brands to assess their congruence with needs, expected values, and competitive benefits. During the primary appraisal consumers also evaluate brand strengths and opportunities. In a secondary appraisal, consumers consider the adaptability of brand, its deliverables, and performance (Lazarus 1991). The appraisal theory of emotion proposes that emotions are extracted from appraisals of events leading to different opinions of peers and the society. As the popularity of e-commerce has risen to prominence in the 21st century, most consumers are able to appraise multiple brands online and emotionally perceive the brands, products, or services. Cognitive appraisals and emotions are the dominant determinants of online shopping behavior. Online consumers are more likely to disclose personal information when they have positive cognitive appraisals and liking toward the website in terms of safety and confidence (Li et al. 2017).

Attribution Theory

The contemporary marketplace and business strategies have changed the consumers' decision analytics due to complexities in transactions, emergence of brands, new products and services, and abundance of information and routes to market. Hence, consumers believe in consulting fellow consumers, peers, social media, and corporate announcement than making decisions only based on self-reference and experience. Customer-centric companies therefore focus on taking into the confidence of the society, family, and peers to deploy their marketing strategies effectively, instead of approaching individual consumers and dealing one-on-one negotiations. Consumers today adjudge their decision in reference to the vogue, peer concerns, and social status upon analyzing the public and personal information. Such market scenario appears to be close to the attribution theory toward determining the cognitive behavior of consumers. *Attribution theory* deals with how a social perceiver analyzes public information to arrive at causal explanations for making decisions. This theory examines the relationship between the nature of information gathered and the way it has been combined to form a causal judgment (Fiske and Taylor 1991).

In psychological studies, attribution theory explains how and why people explain events as they do. However, attributions comprehend consumer behavior to adopt a brand, product, or service and analyze their experience with it. Internal attribution refers to the process of cause and effect to the consumer needs, personality, and perceived use value. A consumer analyzes the brand behavior and experience of other consumers in the marketplace, and generally relies on internal attributions, such as personality traits, to judge his decision. The external characteristics of consumer attribution widely focus on the social and market effects than the internal attributes and self-congruence. The attribution elements that affect consumer cognition include choice, intentions, social desirability, hedonistic relevance, and congruence to personality. These elements affect short-run perceptions among consumers, and help in developing intentions of brand association. However, to develop long-run brand associations, and build attitude and behavior of consumers toward the brand, the factors concerning consensus, distinctiveness, and consistency of behavior also influence the decision process of consumers (Kelley 1967). In general, attribution elements include internal personality factors, culture, and beliefs, all of which affect the consumer perceptions, attitude, and behavior.

Societal Drivers

Social institutions play significant role in nurturing the cultural heritage, which is reflected in the individual behavior. Such institutions include family, education, and political structures. The media affects the ways in which people relate to one another, organize their activities to live in harmony with one another, teach acceptable behavior to succeeding generations, and govern themselves. The status of gender in society, family, social classes, group behavior, age groups, and the way societies define decency and civility are interpreted differently within every culture. Social institutions are a system of regulatory norms and rules of governing actions in pursuit of immediate ends, in terms of their conformity with the ultimate common value system of a community. They constitute underlying norms and values making up the common value system of a society. Institutions are intimately related to, and derived from, the value attitudes common to members of a community. This establishes institutions as primarily moral phenomena, which leads to enforce individual decisions on all human needs including economic and business-related issues. The primary means for enforcement of norms is the moral authority, whereby an individual obeys the norms because that individual believes that the norm is good for its own sake (Rajagopal, Castaño, and Flores 2016). Consumer behavior is also governed by sociocultural determinants as stated as follows:

- Social values on consumption
- Learned culture effects on consumer preferences
- Community consumption pattern and personality-led preferences
- Gender, geo-demographic, and economic variables affecting the consumption pattern
- Impact of acquired culture on consumerism in the society

Long before children enter school, most have already been socialized into play, social values, behaviors, attitudes and linguistic repertoires shaped by the videogames, television (TV) programs, and spin-off toys. Childhood culture is an imaginary universe, which connects TV programs to movies, videogames, toys, T-shirts, shoes, games, crayons, coloring books, bed linens and towels, pencil cases, lunch boxes, and even wallpaper. Media icons extend to fast food chain or cereal box-top contests and special giveaway deals beyond the merchandise transformations of movie or TV program characters. They are also used in shopping mall entertainments featuring the cartoons Lion King, Ice Age, or Spirit from Walt Disney productions. Contests such as a prize trip to Disney Land to meet the characters create a business platform for the target group though cultural penetrations. TV shapes the child's early age into narrative and consumption styles, and by cross-referencing to other narrative forms such as movies, stories, comic books, videogames, and music videos (often movie soundtracks), of which toys and teens' popular culture are an integral extension. Thus, TV serves as a clearing house for both the verbal communication, and artifacts of consumption. For children, the jump from narrative to commodities from Transformer cartoons to Transformer toys and from Disney cartoons to McDonald's giveaways of characters inculcates the consumption behavior, and forms the cultural base that childhood is experiencing in Western countries. Besides, parents also tend to take their children to a fast-food corner and purchase the latest collectibles, and buy the TV-advertised cereal or peanut butter that children demand, to avoid embarrassing situations in the supermarket. These everyday consumer and social practices constitute social and material relations between parents and children (Livingstone and Helsper 2004).

Cannon–Bard Theory of Emotions

Most consumer products companies are able to create sustainable emotions through brand communications, brand promotions, and peer reviews among consumers. However, yet one major challenge these companies face is to drive consumers to take action in view of the decisions made. Companies need to work beyond communicating successful advertisements and brand communications, and understand the ACCA paradigm toward convergence of awareness, comprehension, conviction, and action (ACCA). To generate emotions among consumers, it is essential to create awareness through substantial comprehension. These factors would be able to build emotions among consumers, and drive intension toward associating with the brand (conviction). This stage is sensitive for both consumers and companies, because most consumers review their decision on brand association and purchase intentions, and tend to seek opinion of other consumers. Reviewing opinion of other consumers might override the self-reference of a consumer and defer the action (Rajagopal

2011). Therefore, companies should ensure that the consumer emotions need to be meticulously escorted through the internal and external factors until consumers enact upon their decision.

The Cannon–Bard theory of emotion, a physiological explanation of emotion developed by Walter Cannon and Philip Bard, states that people feel emotions and experience physiological reactions to it such as sensory responses, neurological stimulus, or arousal simultaneously. Most neuro-marketing studies have revealed that the effect of certain publicity campaigns, brands, and products on consumers develop attention and the emotional engagement, from a cognitive and emotional point of view (Sebastian 2014). The Cannon–Bard theory suggests that the physiological reactions are cognitively labeled and need to be interpreted as a particular emotion. For instance, Nike's advertising through sports celebrities makes the common consumer realize the vigor and turn it on to the head. Instead of inspiring customer loyalty by singling out an external enemy, it focuses on an internal foe, "our laziness." Nike advertising knows just how often we battle with our lazy side and hold our emotions to master in a physical activity or a particular sport. The theory emphasizes the role that cognition and elements of the situation play in the experience of emotion (Cannon 1927).

Consumer Acquisition and Retention Strategies

The traditional approach to customer acquisition involves developing a combination of mass marketing including advertisements in the print and electronic media, and billboards, and direct marketing using telemarketing and direct mail tools. However, firms that involve customers in design, testing, marketing, and the after-sales process get better insights into customer needs and behavior and may be able to cut the cost of acquiring customers, engender greater loyalty, and speed up development cycles. Leveraging and linking systems to automate the processes for answering inquiries from customers dramatically reduce the cost of serving them, while increasing their satisfaction and loyalty. As a result, firms retain the existing customers and acquire new customers. More recently, Carrefour, Metro, Walmart Stores, and other large retailers have adopted digital-tagging technologies, such as radio frequency identification, which helped firms in never letting their store shelves get empty, and to make the products available to customers uninterruptedly. This strategy has developed confidence among customers and strengthened the rate of acquiring new customers for these retailing firms. The multinational retailing firms develop strong information base about the business environment in a marketplace, focus their efforts on adapting to the given consumer preferences and retail environment, and set gradual penetration process in the marketplace. On the contrary, the global retailing firms attempt to acquire customers for the economic reasons of lowering the prices by standardizing their marketing operations (Rajagopal and Castaño 2015). For example, Wal-Mart has emerged, with its everyday low price (ELDP) policy, as one of the most favored retail stores in the price-sensitive developed and developing countries.

Customer acquisition and retention are largely based on the perceptions, corporate strategies, and social recognition of the brand. Companies make continuous efforts to acquire new customers by educating them on the brand performance and promotions, while the existing customers are retained by experience sharing across the spatial and temporal metrics. Bankinter, a relatively small Spanish bank, has a large presence as an Internet financial services provider in the country, who is leading the way to profitability through the Internet operations by delivering major competitive advantage over the established Spanish banks. The company acquires new customers, who tend to defect from other banks. It uses tools such as customer relationship management, activity-based costing, customer profitability, and lifetime customer value to determine the value of new customers for the bank and, in doing so, decides on future customer acquisition strategies (Martinez-Jerez, Narayanan, and Brem 2003).

Contemporary developments in information and communication technologies have brought both opportunities and challenges in the global markets to turn them borderless in business. Accordingly, companies and consumers face a dynamic and interconnected international environment in acquiring, retaining, and valuing their customers. Categorically, successful social strategies of the companies are the ones that reduce costs as well as augment consumers' purchase intentions and willingness to pay, by strengthening relationships with the company. Examples of successful digital marketing companies may be cited as Zynga, eBay, American

Express, and Yelp, which endorse how strategies involving social networks can generate profits. The social media-based digital marketing companies have been successful at acquiring customers, promoting peer-to-peer marketing, and engaging customers in cocreation of digital marketing contents (Piskorski 2011). In general word of mouth is something about how people react to variability in product and service performance within a niche. However, as the communication circles expand, the reach of informal communication enhances at various territorial levels. The customer acquisition, retention, and referrals are cocreated by the consumers and market players associated with the company in the social media platforms. Consumer involvement in social networks and company's external relations helps in developing sustainable customer value. The customer value is an important parameter for the companies to play a defensive role in the marketplace to acquire and retain customers. Building up customer value, involving them in the various products and services from designing to delivery, and serviceability help the companies to gain competitive advantage.

A company in a business market must manage customers individually, understanding their needs (problems) and delivering value (solutions) to create sustainable perception, attitude, and behavior among consumes. Companies can motivate consumers to build loyalty by developing individual relationships with consumers. To achieve these ends, the companies must become aware of the different types of competitive advantages and convey their values appropriately to the consumers. As customers become increasingly loyal, they display behaviors in a predictable sequence, exhibiting the relationship and providing word-of-mouth endorsements (Narayandas 2005).

Customers can be retained by a firm by making the customer value apparent while carrying transactions. A firm need to analyze the net benefit it can expect from a customer at the point of sales. Therefore, the firm would like to form some expectation regarding the lifetime value of that customer at various points of transactions. This expectation can then be used to make marketing activities more efficient and effective. It is observed that the retribution of customer retention is customer defection, although customers offer maximum market information by signaling ineffective strategies in acquisition and retention. Learning these inefficiencies forces a firm to shift retention expenditures from low- to high-value customers. Customer recovery strategies dissuade customers, who are likely to switch. The ongoing process of customer loss means that the total group of customers, who left a brand, grows in number every year, and can form a substantial part of the market. Moreover, given the total number of "good" customers or the customers with a sufficient lifetime value in the market is limited, brand managers might not be able to afford to forget and ignore their lapsed customers, in the hope of replacing them with the new ones. Knowing how lapsed customers are likely to react in response to their former brand in the future is useful for targeting and reacquisition strategies.

Most consumer-centric companies have made an aggressive shift in customer acquisition strategies from conventional to digital platforms. Rather than a broad conventional customer acquisition approach, most companies use business-to-consumer e-commerce, and focus on highly segmented digital acquisition marketing. By analyzing customer needs, for example, based on referral paths, search terms, conversion rates, industries, and geographies, companies tend to identify the best prospects and customize their user experience with personalized messaging, pathways, offers, and so on. Companies employing these tactics are achieving twice the revenue growth rates, triple the customer growth rates, and 30 percent higher acquisition efficiency than those businesses that deploy the traditional sales model (Avrane-Chopard et al. 2014). Companies today are commonly engaged in following strategies to acquire customers and retain the existing customers:

- Driving consumer lifetime value through deep cognitive analytics
- Optimizing loyalty programs
- Enhancing customer experience and developing consistency in attitude-behavior of customers

Companies build integrated, cross-functional programs through an in-depth understanding of affinity and traction in relation to new and existing customers. At this stage companies often struggle to deliver sustainable customer value, and strive to reach higher level of behavioral analytics to understand cognitive enhancements of customers, and act accordingly.

Companies in hospitality industry determine the consumer lifetime value by using customer insights to overhaul an outmoded loyalty program, and retain the existing customers. Similarly, retail banks recovered their annual credit losses and customer defection to competing financial institutions, by building an early intervention strategy to minimize customer defaults.

To acquire new consumers and retain their partisans, companies should hire new types of talent, move away from outdated measures of success, and become adept at rapid test-and-learn strategies. A successful omni-channel strategy not only guarantees wide outreach of business in today's environment, but also brings out a revolution in customers' expectations and experiences (Rigby 2011). To acquire and maintain loyal customers, e-retailers must build good relationships with their consumers for long-term mutual benefits. Trust is crucial for any long-term business relationship. Good companies advocate for their customers; in turn, customers reciprocate with their trust, loyalty, and purchases. The firms might then command higher prices for its products and services, as many customers will be willing to pay for the extra value. As consumers trust a company, they often act as referrals and advocate its strengths to the community through the social media, helping to reduce the organization's costs for acquiring new customers (Urban 2004).

Consistency Theory

Acquiring and retaining customers have become more challenging today for the consumer products companies, due to the increasing awareness among the consumers about the substitute products. Easy access to awareness about the competitive products and opportunities to experience them widen the choice spread among consumers, which causes inconsistency in the cognitive behavior streamlining perceptions, attitude, and behavior of consumers. The consistency theory focuses on the balance the individuals create cognitively, when inconsistencies cause tensions and motivate the brain and body to respond. This theory is very similar to the cognitive dissonance theory, which emphasizes the importance of positive and negative outcomes to reduce stressful choices. Although the cognitive consistency theory touches this issue, it focuses on the effects of inconsistencies motivating people to react (Festinger 1957).

Commonly for a reputed brand and long-standing consumer products company, beliefs, attitudes, and values of consumers are all aligned with their behavior, as they experience AATAR factors to reach at a comfortable state of affairs. The discomfort of cognitive dissonance occurs when things fall out of alignment due to competitive intervention, innovations, or sharing of new experiences across the consumers. The cognitive dissonance disrupts the consumer balance and drives polarization of choices to existing products and services or those are new and often cause defection of consumers from a brand or company. This challenge is experienced by majority of companies as they find that the market and consumers both are becoming dynamic and inconsistent today. Companies can achieve consistency between conflicting cognition by streamlining the consumer perceptions and attitudes, understanding the following cognitive imperatives:

- Denial: *I didn't see it happen*—consumers defect from the brand when it did not live up to their expectation. Such perception might cause for two reasons—either consumers did not have adequate knowledge, or they did not get desired customer support from the company.
- Rationalization and excuses: *It was going to happen anyway*—stating preconceived justification for the success or failure. Consumers exhibit such behavior when they value or reject their decision. However, companies need to ensure that consumers have high brand literacy, knowledge, use value, and experience to rationalize their decisions rightly. Consumers view brands as extensions of their self-concepts and self-image transmission symbols. Sometimes consumer-brand relationships have a presence of negative brand information, for example, negative publicity, brand rumors, product-harm crises, and so on, which affects unfavorable postpurchase comparisons with the competing products (Davvetas and Diamantopoulos 2017).

- Usability: *I don't use my car enough to make a difference*—some consumers buy products as status symbol in the society but do not get adequately associated with it due to discrete usability. Under such circumstances it is difficult for consumers to develop consistency in attitude and behavior, though they might hold high perceived value for the product. The luxury car companies like BMW always pursue their customers in the emerging markets to have second BMW in their family, as the company would like to inculcate the association with the brand and develop attitude of consumers to stay with the brand, instead of just considering it as a societal status symbol.

- Transcendence: *Nobody is perfect*—transcendence behavior among consumers reveals that they expect high perfection, even beyond practicality. Such perception leads to dissatisfaction and to a general conclusion to draw cognitive balance, as no product can deliver total satisfaction. Transcendence behavior is often observed among consumers as a "compromise" with the existing products and services. Such complexities in the behavior of consumers are very hard for companies to resolve. Thus, most companies face a category of hard consumers or laggards, who always defer decisions because of transcendence behavior. The widespread word of mouth, positive psychodynamics, involvement of consumers in social media, digital space attractions, and attractive public profiles of companies could help companies to streamline the transcendence behavior of consumers. Creating self-knowledge, self-actualization, and self-enhancement among consumers and developing transformational leadership through customer relationship strategies would also help companies to reform such consumer behavior (Lönnqvist et al. 2011).

- Leaning toward defection: *I will be more careful next time*— transcendence behavior, partial dissatisfaction, compromising behavior, and peer interventions drive the consumers to lean toward defection. Leaning toward frequent changes exhibits inconsistency in behavior among consumers, and poses a major challenge for the companies to retain these consumers. Consumer-centric companies should improve their customer relations strategies by enhancing the scope of value streams and persuasion to retain the consumers.

- Self-actualization: *I am good, really, am I not?* This cognitive situation often occurs to many consumers, when they are indecisive to justify their actions. Behavioral consistency of consumers is affected as they fail to succeed self-actualization and justify their decisions. One of the effective strategies for companies to help consumers to achieve self-actualization is to provide attractive celebrity endorsement on brands so that consumers can personify the brand and evangelize self-image.

Human personality traits are determined by multidimensional factors like the individual's behavior, appearance, attitude and beliefs, and demographic characteristics. Based on the trait theory, researchers have concluded that there are five stable personality dimensions, also called the "Big Five" human personality dimensions. The Big Five factors include extroversion, agreeableness, conscientiousness, neuroticism, and openness to experience. Relationship between the point of sales promotions and retail-buying decisions is largely governed by the psychographic variables that can be measured broadly by the closeness and farness of the personalities of brand and customer. The type of relationship that customers possess with the point of sales promotions offered by retail stores is largely based on the loyalty levels. The new-generation marketing approaches include customer focused, market-driven, outside-in, one-to-one marketing, data-driven marketing, relationship marketing, integrated marketing, and integrated marketing communications that emphasize two-way communication through better listening to customers and the idea that communication before, during, and after transactions can build or destroy important brand relationships (Rajagopal and Castaño 2015).

Variety-Seeking Behavior

Variety seeking has been observed in many consumer products, and it has been identified as a key determinant factor in brand switching. This type of behavior is explained by experiential or hedonic motives rather than by utilitarian aspects of consumption. Among the range of various strategies available to a company, line extensions are an important way to keep a brand alive and to realize incremental financial growth. Of all line extensions, those involving new flavors and new packaging/sizes are most successful. Extensions that improved product quality were found to be unsuccessful. The market variables such as level of competition, retailer power, and variety-seeking behavior showed a negative influence on line extension success. The behavior of variety seeking among the consumers has been divided into derived or direct variations. Consumer behavior emerging out of external or internal forces that have no concern with a preference for change in, and of, itself may be referred as derived varied behavior. Direct varied behavior has been defined in reference to "novelty," "unexpectedness," "change," and "complexity" as they are pursued to gain inherent satisfaction. In a study, the influence of product-category level attributes was examined, and six influential factors including involvement, purchase frequency, perceived brand difference, hedonic feature, and strength of preference and purchase history have been identified. Innovative concept of market entry strategy is based on moving with consumer space, which indicates that foreign firms enter the destination market by developing adequate consumer awareness on the products and services prior to launch. This strategy is followed largely by the fast-moving consumer goods manufacturing companies, and such practice is termed as go-to-market strategy. Go-to-market planning enables the firm to achieve higher margins, accelerated revenue growth, and increased customer satisfaction through existing sales channels. An effective go-to-market strategy aligns products and services, processes, and partners with customers and markets to deliver brand promise, the desired customer experience, and tangible value. The go-to-market strategy services help technology suppliers overcome market challenges (Rajagopal 2010b).

Choice Theory

Choice theory suggests contemporary explanation to the variety-seeking behavior of consumers in the competitive marketplace today. A central aspect of the theory is the belief that we are internally, not externally, motivated. It suggests that outside events never make us to do anything. What drive our behavior are internally developed notions of what is most important and satisfying to us. With regard to consumer behavior, the perceived use value, value for money, self-actualization, personification of brands, and brand association are the internal judgments that drive consumers make choices. However, in a marketplace with growing competitive products and services of identical and similar attributes, the external influence on the variety-seeking behavior cannot be ignored. When consumers have no competing or substitutable product or service, they have no choices except to stay with the one available. Such situation may not necessarily be an internal choice of the consumer, but a compromise leading to dissatisfaction in the long run. The choice or variety-seeking behavior among consumers in a competitive marketplace has a strong external influence driven by the information and experience sharing, innovation and technology, corporate image and brand equity, and sustainable use value among other consumers. The cognitive determinants that influence the variety-seeking behavior of consumers include information support, internal and external encouragement, word-of-mouth dynamics, acceptability, trust, reputation, and negotiable differences (Rajagopal 2015).

Theories of consumer behavior often postulate that consumers make conscious decisions about the brands, products, or services they purchase and use. It is assumed that consumer decisions are preceded by an explicit formation of attitudes and needs that determine the brand of choice. However, research from the domain of automaticity proposes that the majority, if not all, of human behavior either begins as an unconscious process, or occurs completely outside of conscious awareness. These automatic processes, including behavioral mimicry, trait and stereotype activation, and nonconscious goal pursuit, also impact attitudes, beliefs, and goals without engaging consumers' conscious minds, which are completely controlled by contextual stimuli (Neale and Kyle 2011).

Rational choice theory describes rationality of consumer choice as a conventional, learned, acquired, or shared wisdom in making buying decisions toward products and services, considering the comparative advantages in the value for money. The rationality associated with the consumer choice in business is different from the colloquial and most philosophical use of the word that typically denotes rationality as sane or thoughtful. The rational choice theory uses a specific and narrower definition of rationality explaining that individuals act in the buying process for balancing costs against benefits to arrive at action that maximizes personal advantage. It also suggests that consumers with a strong self-reference criterion exhibit independent and measurable decisions in the market. Thus, rationality is seen as patterns of choices, rather than of individual perceptions.

Rational choices of consumers can be explained as reversible decisions in case of the risk of delivering low value, in comparison to alternate decisions. In rational choice process, individuals are seen motivated by the needs, which offer options for strategic or tactical decision making. Consumers in the present digital era act within the community, and develop their preferences by analyzing the given information on the products and services. Rational choices hold that individuals must anticipate the outcomes of alternative courses of action and calculate that which will be best for them. Rational consumers choose the alternative that is likely to give them the greatest satisfaction. The rational decision of consumers generally not only implies to an individual consumer, but also works as a conscious preferential move in a social actor engaging in community strategies. The behavior of consumers is shaped by the gains and losses that emerge as a consequence of their involvement in decision making. Reinforcement of right consumer choices through gainful promotions of products and services needs to be technically driven by the companies as conditioning in driving positive attitude among consumers (Homans 1961).

Cognitive Appraisal Theory

Consumers' emotions are extracted from appraisals, estimates, or evaluations of events that cause specific reactions in different people. Essentially, appraisal of a situation causes an emotional response, which stimulates the consumer choice and ability to make decisions. Cognitive appraisals are based on an event, brand, product, or service, which consumers evaluate to make decisions. Such appraisals lead to critical thinking and cognitive arousal among consumes guiding them further on making appropriate decisions. For example, which shopping, when consumers find the environment significantly positive, exhibits higher impulse buying behaviors and experiences enhanced satisfaction. The retail self-service stores that largely operate in chain are based on the rationale of *touch, feel, and pick,* which provides consumers a wide range of options to make buying decisions. The in-stores promotions and do-it-yourself opportunities constitute the major motivation for the buyers and also support their decision-making process (Rajagopal 2009). The cognitive appraisal process is formed in a linear model comprising "situation-thinking-emotions-reactions."

Visual effects associated with products often stimulate the buying decisions among young consumers. Point of sales brochures, catalogs, and posters build assumption on perceived use value and motivational relevance of buying decisions of product. Emotional visuals exhibited on contextual factors such as proximity or stimulus size drive perception and subjective reactions on utility and expected satisfaction of the products (Codispoti and De Cesarei 2007). Consumers generally carry on appraisals in three levels—primary appraisal, secondary appraisal, and reappraisal. In primary appraisal, consumers tend to analyze a brand, retail environment, or a business situation in reference to stimulus–response being positive, stressful, or irrelevant to well-being. In secondary appraisal, consumers evaluate the resources to match their purchase intentions for acquiring the product or service. Consumers seek opinion of other users to reappraise their perceptions and validate decisions. These forms of appraisal involve deliberate conscious processing. An augmented and sustainable customer value builds loyalty toward the product and the brand. Systematically explored customer preferences, and arousal-driven retailing approach toward new products, would be beneficial for a company to derive long-term profit optimization strategy over the period.

Conversion Theory

Most consumers prefer to homogenize their decision by influencing others to follow their decision, or to thrust their perceptional model on other consumers. Such cognitive drive can be described as the focus of conversion theory in reference to consumer behavior. By doing so, consumers validate their decision, and apprehend lower risk of failure. "Me too" feeling is a positive side of conversion, while the negative aspect of such conversion drive is to get into a niche along with others, and convince self-appraisal that "it happens to everyone." The power of such consumers, who try to convert others into their own cognitive response niche, exhibits consistency, confidence, unbiased attitude, and resistance to change. Accordingly, the theory explains that, in groups, the minority can have a disproportionate effect, converting many "majority" members to their own cause. Consumer-centric companies, therefore, attempt to develop a uniform stimulus–response paradigm and perceptional value, and provide undifferentiated information for brand appraisal to categories of consumers.

Routes to Market

Information technology is undergoing a relentless shift with the advances toward virtualization, grid computing, and web services that are enabling the companies to grow their business in customer-centric platforms and gain competitive advantage in the marketplace. The virtualization of business has passed through three stages in reaching the business pattern of today, where a consumer feels that he has access to the company from products to the stakeholder rights. First, home computers and e-mail spawned as the tools of freelancing and offering both consumers and companies to demonstrate new flexibilities, followed by the mobile technology, which gave the 360° business access—anywhere and shop anytime flexibility to the consumers. Now, in a third wave of technology, new ways of providing community opportunity in involving business and sharing thinking space are driving the effect of virtualization through increased consumer–company collaboration (Johns and Gratton 2013). Virtualization enables personal computing platforms to run applications designed on one operating system to be deployed elsewhere. Grid computing allows large numbers of hardware components such as servers or disk drives to effectively act as a single device, pooling their capacity and allocating it automatically to different jobs, while web services standardize the interfaces between applications, turning them into modules that can be assembled and disassembled easily (Carr 2005).

With the appearance of dot-com bubble during the end of 20th century, the online retailers regained confidence, and got engaged in pushing their business to the following century. E-commerce is experiencing encouraging growth today and has appeared as a strong omni-channel. Among all available physical marketing channels, digital retailing is now considered as highly profitable. As virtual shopping options and technology-led routes to markets are evolving, digital retailing is quickly morphing into omni-channel retailing. This channel reflects the fact that retailers will be able to interact with customers through numerous routes to markets consisting of physical stores, kiosks, direct mail and catalogs, call centers, social media, mobile devices, gaming consoles, televisions, networked appliances, home services, and more. As traditional retailers with the brick-and-mortar stores continue despite the boom of virtual shops, they must embrace omni-channel retailing and transform to compete with the Internet-based retailers as consumers tend to shift their shopping behaviors. They must turn shopping into an entertaining, exciting, and emotionally engaging experience by skillfully blending the physical with the digital. To acquire new consumers and retain their partisans, companies should hire new kinds of talent, move away from outdated measures of success, and become adept at rapid test-and-learn strategies. A successful omni-channel strategy not only guarantees wide outreach of business in today's environment but also brings out a revolution in customers' expectations and experiences (Rigby 2011).

Recent technology has advanced beyond e-commerce to m-commerce through various applications for mobile devices and augmented reach of retailing companies and consumer access, bridging traditional and Internet retailing. Such synchronization of routes to markets has enabled retailers to interact with consumers through multiple touchpoints and expose them to a rich blend of offline sensory information and online content. In the past, brick-and-mortar retail stores were unique in allowing consumers to touch and feel merchandise, and provide instant gratification. Internet retailers tried to woo shoppers as the technology has supported the consumer-buying platforms with wide product selection, low prices, and contents such as product reviews and ratings. Such development has pushed retailers and their supply chain partners in other industries to rethink their competitive strategies. The growing prevalence of location-based applications on mobile devices has provided an unprecedented pull effect of consumers to the retail industry. The pull factors have driven the retailers to low-cost online advertising linked to the routine surf and search process on the Internet. Google has made the advertisements still economical for the retailer through their "pay per click" policy. Mobile technology has emerged as a strong change agent to the consumer behavior and expectations. By giving consumers more accurate information about product availability in local stores, retailers can draw people into stores who might otherwise have only looked for products online. The enhanced search capability is especially helpful with niche products, which are not always available in local stores. The availability of market information, the ability of consumers to shop online and pick up products in local stores, and the aggregation of offline information and online content have combined to make the retailing landscape increasingly competitive. In an omni-channel world there is a premium for retailers on learning rapidly from consumers and catering to their needs (Brynjolfsson, Hu, and Rahman 2013). Most customer-centric companies are trying to increase customer loyalty, marketing efficiency, and brand performance by building communities on the virtual platforms around their brands. However, it appears to be a complex strategy as it is often difficult to understand what brand communities are required to drive the market share and how they work in an increasingly growing competition.

Summary

Consumer behavior is a process developed through perceptions for long-term and sustainable attitude over time. The cognitive dimension of consumers can be understood, and the means-end decision process can be defined, by the process of perception-attitude-behavior. Several motivational theories discussed in this chapter reveal that consumers often face many complex cognitive situations, which do not give a clear understanding to the companies to develop appropriate strategies. Consumers undergo acquiescence bias within peers and develop acquired needs, a "me too" feeling, of which companies take advantage in developing proconsumer marketing strategies. Customer-centric companies drive motivational push to activate consumer needs and actions to enable them in developing the right decision. It may be learned from the discussion in this chapter that activation theory describes how cognitive arousal is necessary for effective functioning of people and obtaining expected satisfaction. In addition, cognitive and physical convergence effects exhibit a symbiotic relationship between mind and body movements. This chapter has also addressed consumer ecosystem, decision appraisal, and attribution theories, in addition to the consumer emotions theories. The strategies for consumer acquisition and retention and theories associated with variety-seeking behavior have also been the focal discussion in this chapter, which enhances the learning on various dimensions of consumer behavior.

References

Avrane-Chopard, J., T. Bourgault, A. Dubey, and L. Moodley. 2014. *Big Business in Small Business: Cloud Services for SMBs*. New York, NY: McKinsey & Company, Inc.

Bee, C., and D.O. Neubaum. 2014. "The Role of Cognitive Appraisal and Emotions of Family Members in the Family Business System." *Journal of Family Business Strategy* 5, no. 3, pp. 323–33.

Belanche, D., C. Flavián, and A. Pérez-Rueda. 2014. "The Influence of Arousal on Advertising Effectiveness." In *Proceedings of Measuring Behavior*, Wageningen, The Netherlands, August 27–29.

Brynjolfsson, E., Y.J. Hu, and M.S. Rahman. 2013. "Competing in the Age of Omnichannel Retailing." *Sloan Management Review* 54, no. 4, pp. 23–29.

Cannon W.B. 1927. "The James-Lange Theory of Emotions: A Critical Examination and an Alternative Theory." *American Journal of Psychology* 39, nos. 1–4, pp. 106–24.

Carr, N.G. 2005. "End of Corporate Computing." *Sloan Management Review* 46, no. 3, pp. 67–73.

Codispoti, M., and A. De Cesarei. 2007. "Arousal and Attention: Picture Size and Emotional Reactions." *Psychophysiology* 44, no. 5, pp. 680–86.

Davvetas, V., and A. Diamantopoulos. 2017. "'Regretting Your Brand-Self?' The Moderating Role of Consumer-Brand Identification on Consumer Responses to Purchase Regret." *Journal of Business Research* 80, no. 7, pp. 218–27.

Festinger, L. 1957. *A Theory of Cognitive Dissonance*. Stanford, CA: Stanford University Press.

Fiske, S.T., and S.E. Taylor. 1991. *Social Cognition,* 2nd ed. New York, NY: McGraw-Hill.

Homans, G. 1961. *Social Behaviour: Its Elementary Forms*. London, UK: Routledge and Kegan Paul.

Johns, T., and L. Gratton. 2013. "The Third Wave of Virtual Works." *Harvard Business Review* 91, no. 1, pp. 66–73.

Kelley, H.H. 1967. "Attribution Theory in Social Psychology." In *Nebraska Symposium on Motivation*, ed. D. Levine, 192–238. 15 Vols. Lincoln, NE: University of Nebraska Press.

Lazarus, R.S. 1991. "Progress on a Cognitive-Motivational-Relational Theory of Emotion." *American Psychologist* 46, no. 8, pp. 819–34.

Li, H., X. Luo, J. Zhang, and H. Xu. 2017. "Resolving the Privacy Paradox: Toward a Cognitive Appraisal and Emotion Approach to Online Privacy Behaviors." *Information & Management* 54. http://dx.doi.org/10.1016/j.im.2017.02.005

Livingstone, S., and E. Helsper. 2004. "Advertising 'Unhealthy' Foods to Children: Understanding Promotion in the Context of Children's Daily Lives." Research Department of the Office of Communications, London School of Economics, Working Paper, April.

Lönnqvist, J.E., G. Walkowitz, M. Verkasalo, and P.C. Wichardt. 2011. "Situational Power Moderates the Influence of Self-Transcendence vs. Self-Enhancement Values on Behavior in Ultimatum Bargaining." *Journal of Research in Personality* 45, no. 3, pp. 336–39.

Martinez-Jerez, A.F., V.G. Narayanan, and L. Brem. 2003. *Internet Customer Acquisition Strategy at Bankinter*. Cambridge, MA: Harvard Business School Press.

McClelland, D.C. 1978. "Managing Motivation to Expand Human Freedom." *American Psychologist* 33, no. 3, pp. 201–10.

Narayandas, D. 2005. "Building Loyalty in Business Markets." *Harvard Business Review* 83, no. 9, pp. 131–39.

Neale, M., and M. Kyle. 2011. "Unconscious Mental Processes in Consumer Choice: Toward a New Model of Consumer Behavior." *Journal of Brand Management* 18, no. 7, pp. 483–505.

Piskorski, M.J. 2011. "Social Strategies that Work." *Harvard Business Review* 48, no. 3, pp. 247–53.

Rajagopal., and R. Castaño. 2015. *Understanding Consumer Behaviour and Consumption Experience*. Hershey, PA: IGI Global.

Rajagopal. 2009. "Arousal and Merriment as Decision Drivers among Young Consumers." *Journal of International Consumer Marketing* 21, no. 4, pp. 271–83.

Rajagopal. 2010a. "Interdependence of Personality Traits and Brand Identity in Measuring Brand Performance." *International Journal of Business Innovation and Research* 4, no. 5, pp. 411–26.

Rajagopal. 2010b. *Consumer Behavior: Global Shifts and Local Effects*. Hauppauge, New York, NY: Nova Science Publishers Inc.

Rajagopal. 2011. "Impact of Radio Advertisements on Buying Behaviour of Urban Commuters." *International Journal of Retail and Distribution Management* 39, no. 7, pp. 480–503.

Rajagopal. 2015. *Butterfly Effect in Competitive Markets: Driving Small Change for Larger Differences*. Basingstoke, Hampshire, UK: Palgrave Macmillan.

Rajagopal., R. Castaño, and D. Flores. 2016. *Consumer and Markets: Analyzing Behavioral Shifts and Emerging Challenges*. Hauppauge, New York, NY: Nova Publishers.

Rigby, D. 2011. "The Future of Shopping." *Harvard Business Review* 85, no. 12, pp. 65–76.

Sebastian, V. 2014. "Neuromarketing and Evaluation of Cognitive and Emotional Responses of Consumers to Marketing Stimuli." *Procedia—Social and Behavioral Sciences* 127, pp. 753–57.

Uduji, J.I., and M.O. Ankeli. 2013. "Needs for Achievement, Affiliation, and Power: the Possible Sales Manager's Actions for Exceptional Salesforce Performance." *Research Journal of Finance and Accounting* 4, no. 9, pp. 96–103.

Urban, G.L. 2004. "Emerging Era of Customer Advocacy." *Sloan Management Review* 45, no. 2, pp. 77–82.

Verma, H.V., and E. Duggal. 2015. "Environmental Concerns, Behavior Consistency of Emerging Market: Youth and Marketing." *Emerging Economy Studies* 1, no. 2, pp. 171–87.

Young, S., and F. Barbara. 1975. "Using the Benefit Chain for Improved Strategy Formulation." *Journal of Marketing* 39, no. 3, pp. 72–74.

Zeithaml, V.A. 1988. "Consumer Perception of Price, Quality, and Value: A Means-End Model and Synthesis of Evidences." *Journal of Marketing* 52, no. 3, pp. 2–22.

CHAPTER 3

Decision Metrics for Competitive Business

Overview

Decision making is a cognitive process for consumers, and an organizational process for the companies to take decisions on developing marketing strategies. Several factors affect the decision process for both consumers and companies, which often make the decision grid complicated. This chapter discusses selective decision theories including social learning and instructional learning theories, drive and cue theories, and optimal distinctiveness theory in the context of consumer behavior and managerial implications. Besides theoretical discussions, this chapter also discusses exogenous and endogenous elements affecting consumer cognition and behavior, convergence of stimuli and response of consumers, and critical indicators of consumer value and loyalty as drivers of consumer decision metrics.

Value Propositions

The customer value concept is utilized to evaluate the product differentiation, and to determine the competitive structure of the new products. The analytical approach to the new product-market structure based on customer value may be fitted well within the microeconomic framework. The measure of customer value as the product efficiency may be viewed from the customer's perspective toward a ratio of outputs (e.g., perceived use value, resale value, reliability, safety, comfort) that customers obtain from a product relative to inputs (price, running costs) that customers must deliver in exchange. The derived efficiency value is the return on the customer's investment. Products offering a maximum customer value relative to all other alternatives in the market are characterized as efficient. Different efficient products may create value in different ways using different strategies (output–input combinations). Each efficient product can be viewed as a benchmark for a distinct submarket. Jointly, these products form the efficient frontier, which serves as a reference function for the inefficient products (Bauer et al. 2004). Thus, customer value of new products is defined as a relative concept. Market partitioning is achieved endogenously by clustering products, which are benchmarked by the peers, in one segment. This ensures that only products with a similar output–input structure are partitioned into the same submarket. As a result, a submarket consists of highly substitutable products. The individual values of the customer are estimated in general as base values, and changes in such values are affected by the corresponding measures of the specific value drivers. The base value ties to the most important of all complements determined as customers' need. Estimating value drivers for a new product can be tricky because there is no direct historical data. However, it can be assumed that the impact from changes in price or availability of complements is similar to what other markets have experienced.

One of the principal requirements for managing the multicultural consumer segments is localization of business. Consumers of diverse cultural segments demand high customization of products and services to suit their culture-oriented consumption patterns. Customization has been a powerful strategy against standardization in consumer markets. Diversity attempts to build stores in attractive locations and customization of products and services, and often meet fierce consumer demands in the market. Companies catering to the consumers in multicultural segments are also engaged in dictating the patterns of standardizations in products and services, and even culturally guiding the architectural styles of new shops to fit into the tastes of consumers of diverse cultural backgrounds. Despite several integrated efforts, it is often hard for the companies to customize every element of customer preferences in different locations. Thus, strategists have begun to use clustering techniques to simplify and smooth out the consumer decision-making process. The typology of consumer culture suggests that learned culture that grows along the society over a long period is highly sustainable and embedded in the consumer behavior. Such culture also represents conventionalism in the consumer decisions (Rajagopal and Castaño 2015).

Decision Theories

Decision process of consumers is a continuous process, which involves internal and external influencing attributes, business situations, degree of complexity, and management of decisions. Consumer decisions vary over the spatial, temporal, socioeconomic, cultural, political, and legal (regulated) market environments besides the corporate policies that influence the decision-making process among consumers. The decision process begins with need identification based on the existing or potential problem. This initial step is the guiding driver for the entire decision process of consumers. If consumers identify a right problem, they can lead to a right need, and move on with the decision process to get the right product for desired satisfaction. However, several intervening factors influence the decision process during the course of time. Most consumers with adequate skills on information analytics organize the decision-making process into four simple steps comprising prodecision, conflicts, risks, and trade-offs of any given situation under which they make the decision. Intrinsic and extrinsic factors affecting the consumer decision process have been exhibited in Figure 3.1 and discussed in the following sections.

In general, the consumer decision process has a linear path of need identification, choosing a right decision driver, examining the decision taken (decision pilot), and approving the decision, as exhibited in Figure 3.1. Need identification is a complex process, which moves ahead

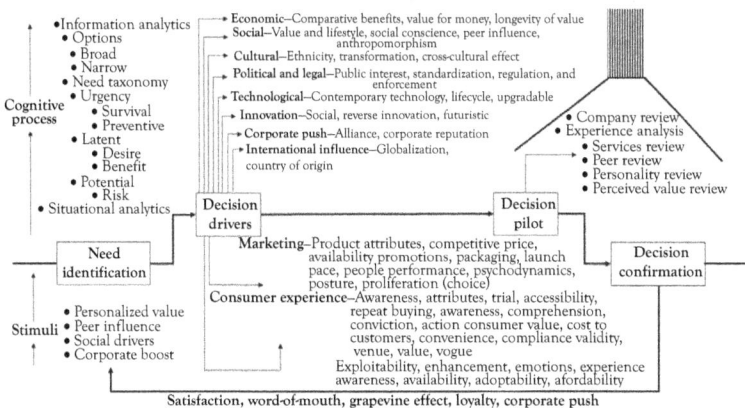

Figure 3.1 Cognitive and strategy map of consumer decision process

as the problem is recognized by the consumers upon analyzing the situation. Accordingly, need is determined within the cognitive taxonomy of urgency, latent, or potential. The urgency of needs drives consumers to make quick decisions, while the latent needs reveal that needs of consumers are pending for a favorable solution. Consumers identify potential needs with an intention to avoid risks in future and ensure their safety. Upon discovering the right need to fit appropriately to the recognized problem, consumers tend to seek solutions from the array of available options and analyze relevant information. Companies provide adequate stimuli through the corporate boost comprising brand campaigns, promotions, social media interactions, peer reviews, and augmented personalized values, to support the cognitive process of consumers. Further, with the cognitive perceptions on the recognized problems and classified needs, consumers tend to evaluate appropriate decision drivers, which are spread across various indicators including economic, social, cultural, political and legal, technological, innovation, corporate, international influence, marketing, and consumer experience. The decision drivers help consumers to formalize their intention and lean toward reviewing the perceived value on various parameters. This stage may be called decision pilot, which, upon satisfactory review, leads to the decision confirmation. Most consumers feel proud of their decision if they succeed in achieving desired satisfaction, and mobilize positive word of mouth in the society, which helps in stimulating the needs of other consumers.

There are several consumer behavior theories that predict how consumers make purchase decisions and show marketers how best to capitalize on predictable behaviors. Though impulse purchases are a significant part of a consumer's buying patterns, rational decision-making processes dominate consumer behavior and affect marketing strategies. The following text discusses important theories on consumer decision making from the point of applied perspectives in marketing management.

Social Learning Theory

In the age of advanced information, technology, and access to the digital space, consumers interact and learn from the experience of each other, and evaluate public opinions before taking any decision. The social learning theory argues that people learn from one another through observation, imitation, and modeling. The theory has often been called a bridge between behaviorist and cognitive learning theories because it encompasses attention, memory, and motivation as strong drivers of learning (Bandura 1977a). More than the digital space, television plays a significant role in learning among young consumers. In society, many influential models, such as family and friends, television, peers, and teachers at schools, colleges, and universities, surround consumers. These models provide examples of behavior to observe and imitate, for example, masculine and feminine celebrities, innovative leaders, or ecological advocates. Young consumers pay attention to some of these models and encode their behavior. Later they may imitate the behavior, sometimes regardless of whether the behavior is "gender appropriate" or not. But a copied behavior can be reproduced in a way deemed appropriate by the society. For example, consumers are influenced by "unisex" clothes or fashion accessories as they attempt to copy brand ambassadors and celebrities.

Besides imitation or copying dimension of the learning process, consumers also learn from the observations in the society, marketplaces, and their workplace. Often consumers seek endorsement from peers, family, or social representatives, during the decision process. Observational learning occurs through observing the behavior of others. It is a form of social learning, which embeds in individual and group behavior. Observational learning could occur when cognitive processes are active in a person. These mental factors intervene (mediate) in the learning process to determine if a new response for decision process is needed (Bandura 1977b). Significant influencing factors that drive the consumers' propensity to observe include consumer risk aversion, brand performance, self-confidence, and living to the expectation to conform to self and group norms (Simpson, Siguaw, and Cadogan 2008). Additionally, moderating effects are identified, indicating that propensity to observe is higher when certain contingencies interact. The mediational factors discussed as follows streamline the observations of a person and help in processing decisions:

Attention: attention emerges as a cognitive driver when a specific behavior is observed, for example, when a performer in a retail store promotes the products through audio-visual entertainment.

Such an event builds the attention of consumers, which they might retain and reproduce as memory at the times of need. Observational learning is therefore a process having convergence with human attention to a specific behavior. Behavior-driven attention may also be used as a source to imitate or reproduce the learning (Bandura 1985). Consumers observe many behaviors in routine of which some lead to top-of-the-mind while others are discarded and might not be reproduced. Attention is therefore an extremely important constituent of consumer behavior, which affects the decision process. A study reveals that consumers spend more time looking at printed communications than those online and through interpersonal exchanges. Among other sources of communications, mobile communications hold customers' attention longer (Greenyer 2008).

Retention: consumers observe many verbal, nonverbal, and visual behaviors but pay attention to few, which are significant to their existing, latent, or potential needs. Accordingly, they analyze observations and categorically store them as top-of-the-mind active memory. Consumers today use digital devices to record their observations, digitize them, and retrieve them whenever necessary. The increasing availability and popularity of the ways to capture personal memories using technologies, such as digital camera, are beginning to alter the way in which personal memory images are produced, retained, and circulated (Mitra 2005).

Retrieval: to support the decision process, consumers tend to retrieve their memories. It is argued that faster retrieval of memories not only streamlines the decision process but also helps consumers in justifying their decision based on their observations.

Motivation: observation of consumers is motivated by peers or self-reference. Upon analyzing the fit of observations to the perceived needs, consumers form memories categorically, and use them in taking appropriate decisions. Accordingly, consumers justify their perceptions, attitude, and behavior. Motivation significantly influences learning and memory. Companies tend to use motivation, cognition, emotions, and responses of the consumers to manage their perception, attitude, and behavior. Experience of

other consumers, which motivates consumer cognitions and emotions, drives their behavior (Kapoor and Kulshrestha 2009).

In view of the previous discussion it can be argued that most consumers learn by observing the behavior of other consumers including peers,
family, and friends, and analyze their behavioral outcome critically, to
support their decision-making process. Initially, learning occurs among
consumers without a change in behavior. Therefore, most consumer-
centric companies focus brand literacy program through social media
and communities to acquire new consumers. Behavioral scientists argue
that consumer learning exhibits recurring change in behavior due to continuous innovations and the growing competition in the marketplace.
Alternatively, consumers also learn through observation alone but not
necessarily lean toward developing attitude and behavior on their knowledge. However, it is not appropriate for companies to educate consumers
on brands and marketing strategies individually or on a one-on-one basis.
Cognition plays a significant role in consumer learning. Awareness and
expectations of information reinforcement or technological shifts would
drive a major effect on the consumer behavior.

Consumer brand motivations are revealed as a self-interest-centered
phenomenon rather than altruistic. Hence, to enhance scope of brand
marketing, firms must aim to modify perceptions and attitudes of larger
consumer segments by implementing educational marketing campaigns
that reinforce the ethical, environmental, and societal benefits of organic
production (McEachern and McClean 2002). The key challenge for
the firms to market their brand against private labels is to strengthen
individuals' perception of the individual benefits by adding more and
stronger emotional values to corporate brands. An increase in customer
value attributes mainly to an increase in the perceived values of brands in
the market. On the other hand, the price effect measures the value change
caused by adding unfamiliar brands of over-the-counter products to the
existing private labels (Rajagopal 2008). The customer value seemed to
decrease as the prices of the familiar brands increased in a large propor-
tion, and the price increase was most pronounced among the users of new
brands. However, risk aversion has been found to be a major emerging
variable, while involvement and environmental concern are significant in

determining the consumer behavior toward new, unfamiliar brands and private labels (Paladino 2005).

Instructional Learning

Most consumer products companies support consumer cognition and learning process by creating consumer orientation, presentation, and guiding consumers through a structured and guided practice on brands, products, and services. During the orientation phase, companies provide verbal and nonverbal information like brochures, pictures and videos, and sharing product experience. Consumers are provided with the hands-on experience in the stage of presentation. Most companies attract consumers through product demonstrations, illustrations of corporate growth, and projecting the future plans. In this phase, consumers critically analyze their learnings, and share feedback with company and social media. During the last phase of consumer instruction model, companies focus on creating self-confidence, perceived use value, and brand association among consumers. Structured practice and guidance involve companies to carry out consumer advocacy to enhance their knowledge and rationale to support their purchase intentions, brand associations, and decision-making process (Joyce and Weil 2004).

Drive Theory

Cognitive drive is a psychological state of mind that controls the needs, decision process, and emotional touchpoints. The stages of need recognition, information analytics, emotions and arousal, and achieving satisfaction largely form the path of cognitive drive among consumers. In psychology, the drive theory is based on the principle that physiological changes in a person take place when certain needs are not satisfied, and they create a state of stress. When a need is satisfied, the drive is reduced and the organism returns to a state of homeostasis and relaxation. However, considering the positive perspective of the drive theory, it is argued that cognitive drive has facets of both positivity and negativity in consumers, while measuring the extent of satisfaction to their needs. Consumers experience cognitive drive and arousal in both instances discussed earlier. Thus, most consumer products companies engage in inculcating cognitive drive and create positive arousal among consumers to develop purchase intentions, brand associations, and loyalty. The drive theory therefore encompasses the following factors:

- Need
- Process
- Satisfaction

There has been steep growth in several consumer sectors over the last decade (2001 to 2010) such as packaged goods, media, food, and consumer electronics. The proliferation of new brands and products has penetrated in various consumer segments, rapidly intensifying the competition in the marketplace. As the new brands emerge faster in the market, the drive operations for companies turn more complex and expensive to boot or reboot the arousal among consumers. Product, price, promotions, packaging, and psychodynamics are the major cognitive drivers among consumers. Increasing competition and emergences of store and commercial brands have strengthened the power of pricing and packaged goods. Most firms have moved beyond product innovation to emphasize demand innovation, which requires understanding the higher-order needs of consumers, and then creating service and product solutions that directly address those needs. Innovation, technology, price offers, and societal push toward quality of life trigger cognitive drive and arousal among consumers. The experiences of Kraft, Procter & Gamble, and Netflix toward innovation, technology, use value, and value for money have exhibited how consumer companies can prompt cognitive drive among consumers, improve consumer experience, inculcate the sense of brand association and loyalty, and find incremental ways to grow in the competitive marketplace (Dutra, Frary, and Wise 2004). Multinational companies dealing with well-established brands that contribute the proven market share like Coca-Cola use this strategy of inserting advertisements in any media with high frequency in a short span. Such advertising strategy helps in position ing brands of the company distinctively in the market against the competing products, and push them to the top-of-the-mind of consumers.

Cue Theory

In a competitive marketplace when innovation, technology, substitute products, and new brands appear frequently, the perception, attitude, and behavior among consumers are rapidly altered, and inconsistency prevails. In due course, consumers tend to forget their previous experience, brands, and the perceived value, as the new brands dominate. The cue theory argues that forgetting occurs when the right cue is not available for retrieving the memory. When a memory is encoded, it leaves traces in the mind, which is termed as "cue." Strong cues help people to retrieve memories faster, while weak clues need strong evidential support to retrieve. Deep inside the medial temporal lobe is the region of the brain known as the *limbic system*, which is particularly relevant to the processing of memory. The neuro-marketing research reveals that to bring the memories on to the top-of-the-mind, relevant cues make greater contribution to the decision-making process of consumers (Booth and Freeman 2014).

There are two types of cue that can aid recall: context and state. Context cues generate similarity effects. Sometimes consumers can retrieve memories based on just the contextual cues. For example, if a consumer is not in the same place as others when learning, the memory may not be accessible to the affected consumer. Consumer products companies follow "cue" strategy of advertisement in order to show their presence regularly, to enable consumers to always locate the brands on top-of-the-mind, and avoid memory fades or loss. Cue is a long-term advertising strategy to develop positive impact on the consumers. Companies engaged in marketing consumer products, which have reached the stage of maturity in the product lifecycle, use cue strategy in advertising. Accordingly, the products are advertised in any media for a reasonably long period on regular intervals. Such product advertising strategy builds brand image and confidence among consumers toward buying and consumption. To refresh memories, companies reinforce verbal and nonverbal advertisements, visual brands, and visual merchandising using flanker strategies. The flanker advertising strategy adds value to the brand name by inserting prefix words or phrases to the brand name and suffix words or phrases to justify the prefix. For example, Nescafé, a popular soluble coffee brand of Nestlé Company, can be advertised using flanker strategy as "new (prefix) - Nescafé- extra freshness (suffix)."

Neuro-marketing studies reveal that the encoding specificity principle states "the greater the similarity between the encoding event and the retrieval event, the greater the likelihood of recalling the original memory." Cue theory from the cognitive perspectives of consumers can be interpreted also in reference to consistency, utility, and confidence. Cues, such as the smell of cookies baking, smell of perfume/cologne, sound of ice falling into a whiskey tumbler, sight of a bowl of ice cream, and sight of a pack of cigarettes, if demonstrated or shown in a visual advertisement at periodical intervals, not only reinforce brand image but also help consumers in retrieving information easily to the top-of-the-mind.

Cognitive Elements Driving Consumer Response

Consumers are continuously engaged in decision process in the competitive marketplace today. Decision process involves choosing options, making the best fit, pilot testing, experiencing perceived use value, developing purchase intentions, and inculcating attitude and behavior. In view of the rapidly growing innovation, technology, and vogue in the society, consumer products companies tend to influence consumers with new attributes of brands, products, and services, and shift the consumer behavior. However, enforcing continuous change in the consumer behavior is not only cognitively sound for consumers but also an unstable foreground for companies to develop consumer-oriented strategies. Intuitively, it seems wrong that any company should seek to manipulate consumers' behavior. However, companies can be ethically engaged in promoting their product or service without forcing consumers to alter their behavior and accept the product or service despite negative perceived value. Most consumers exhibit assertive behavior to the promotions and advertising campaigns and they will not proceed to try it unless they find that the experience shared by other consumers is worth and convincing. Moreover, unless their first-time trial of the product, service, or practice is positive, they will not try it a second time. Accordingly, consumers reinforce their perceived values, develop attitude, and build behavior over time. However, consumers sometimes prefer to change their behavior voluntarily to maximize happiness, by predicting the emotional consequences, and choose products and services. For example, Zipcar customers share the use of cars

- Family
  - Decision making units
  - Need analysis
- Referrals
  - Consumer advocacy
  - Information gatekeepers
- Socio-economic segments
  - Social status
  - Quality of life determinants
- Distinctive behavior
  - Ethnocentric
  - Personal beliefs and values
- Culture
  - Learned
  - Acquired
  - Shared

- Need recognition
  - Problems
  - Perception
- Attitude–behavior convergence
  - Trust, involvement, and commitment
  - Endorsement, judgments, and value
  - Behavior

- Decision confirmation
  - Satisfaction
  - Loyalty
- Decision appraisal
  - Tangible tests
  - Cognitive affirmation
- Decision process
  - Cognitive perceptions
  - Information analysis
- Perceived value
  - Customer relations
  - Counseling
  - Services
  - Self-reference
- Stimuli
  - Social
  - Corporate
  - Retail

Simulation Response Convergence

Exogenous elements

Cognitive elements and consumer response

Endogenous elements

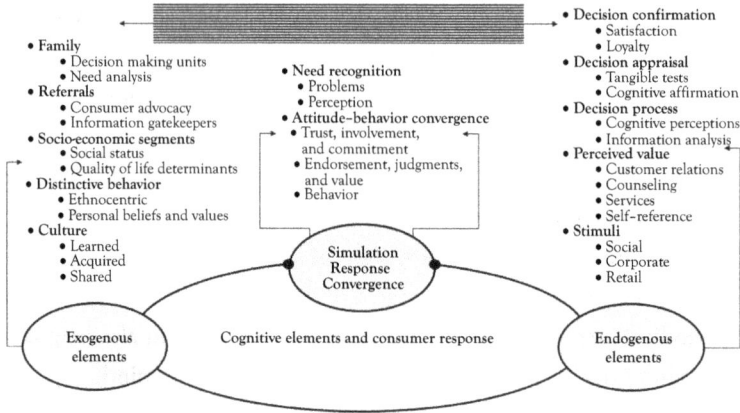

Figure 3.2 Cognitive elements affecting consumer behavior

and, as a result, rely on each other for their service experience. Customers keep the car clean and the gas tank full, and return the car on time. This is a voluntary behavior of consumers to maximize satisfaction. The cognitive elements causing simulation response are exhibited in Figure 3.2 and discussed in the following text.

Exogenous Elements

Culture is the total pattern of behavior that is consistent and compatible in its components. It is not a collection of random behaviors, but behaviors that are related and integrated. It is a learned behavior and not biologically transmitted. It depends on environment, not heredity. It can be called the fabricated part of our environment. A group of people, a society, may manifest the culture in the behavior that is shared. It can be considered as the distinctive way of life of a people. Accordingly, a marketing manager of an international firm is supposed to be familiar with the reference groups, social classes, consumption systems, family structure and decision making, adoption and diffusion, market segmentation, and consumer behavior, in order to understand the cultural environment in the host country.

Often, external cultures influence learned culture and drive consumers toward cross-cultural experience. However, consumers strike a balance between native and acquired cultures and reveal ambidextrous behavior as exhibited in Figure 3.2. Consumers in the acquired culture are prone to behavioral changes, adapt to modern values, and are interactive in the market. These attributes of acquired culture drive multinational companies to develop dynamic marketing strategies, build their brand, and augment market share. Shared culture is an agglomeration of consumers of different cultures in a destination, like the United States, where consumers of Hispanic, Asian, European, and African cultures are located. Such destinations largely induce niche marketing, as consumers prefer to stay with their own cultural regime, though staying overseas. It is commonly observed that the disposable income of consumers in such shared culture markets is limited and they stay price sensitive. Contrary to the shared culture destinations, the interrelated culture provides a wide opportunity to the business houses to expand their manufacturing and marketing operations regionally as there are cultural similarities (Rajagopal 2016).

Culture is perhaps the most fundamental and most pervasive element that influences consumer behavior externally. Culture has social genesis, and it governs various behavioral patterns, ideas, economic and social activities, and consumer preferences today. It evolves over time in reference to the internal and external factors, and moves over generations of consumers. The values of the society tend to be enduring as well. Consumer culture evolves through its distinctive behavioral patterns and values, and transmits them to subsequent generations. The cultural influences on consumer behavior have both tangible and intangible results, such as verbal and nonverbal communications, product attributes, use values, and vogue, as illustrated in Figure 3.2. Basic beliefs, values, preconceived notions, and cognitive assertions that affect consumer behavior are the intangible outcome of the cultural environment. For instance, television culture has deeply engrossed the social culture in India since the 1990s, and it has turned as a lifestyle of people today. Netflix, Inc., the global provider of subscription video on demand, launched its Indian platform in 2016. In view of huge population and embedded television culture in the society, Netflix found India a lucrative market. In addition, the younger generation in India, having dynamic consumption patterns comparable to those of Western consumers, gave this entertainment company another reason to market its products to Indian consumers (Sharma et al. 2017).

Most decisions of consumers are ethnocentric, and are based on cultural norms. Powdered egg had been a breaking innovation in the consumer market during the 1990s, which later expanded to egg flakes. But this product could replace the consumer behavior of eating fresh eggs. Consumer culture has power to accept or reject the innovations and new brands. The prevailing values dictated that a good breakfast from fresh eggs takes time to prepare, while the instant foods and beverages reflect laziness on the part of the user culturally. The latter also reflect carelessness with the household budget, since convenience foods invariably cost more than "natural" foods. Therefore, the consumer perceptions might be resistant to such consumption, and they do not turn into attitude and behavior unless the sociocultural norms shift.

Socioeconomic status is a powerful tool for segmenting consumers and developing marketing strategies as shown in Figure 3.2. Empirical research suggests that people from the same social group tend to have homogeneous needs, preferences, and lifestyles. However, sometime within the same social category, consumers exhibit asymmetric consumption behavior. Thus, the behavior of an individual, on a given occasion, relates to the social role a consumer is playing. In 2015, Puma became the market leader in sportswear sales in India, leaving Adidas, Reebok, and Nike behind. Puma's success in India was primarily attributed to its marketing techniques, judicious expansion, customer segmentation, and acquisition strategy. Indian consumers had been embracing lifestyle changes associated with increased health concerns and the popularity of fitness programs. Such behavior of consumers in the region has been widely homogeneous. Consequently, the sportswear segment grew, presenting an opportunity for companies to maximize their return on investments. While Puma moved ahead of Adidas to become the leading sportswear brand in India, the market evolved and became competitive. Puma needed to continue innovating its marketing strategies to hold onto its leadership position (Puri and Krishna 2016). However, domestic footwear brands were expanding their retail footprints and distribution networks beyond their regional presence to gain a substantial market share and attract consumers using the value for money attribute to drive their perceptions, attitude, and behavior.

Reference groups and gatekeepers also exhibit significant influence on consumer behavior and consumption patterns. In China, the practice of purchasing fish whilst it is still alive is so deeply ingrained that the marketing of frozen fish has barely been established. The reference groups not only keep consumers updated with information but also establish specific norms and values to guide the cognitive process among consumers, and help in making purchase decisions. Most companies use consumer referral groups in developing marketing strategies, not only for acquiring and for retaining consumers but also to inculcate trust, lifetime value, and brand loyalty. Traditional marketing programs seek advocates among current consumers to mobilize word of mouth, and direct managers to aim marketing efforts to create lifetime value for consumers, focus on customer satisfaction, and use social media-based promotional programs. In contrast, referral marketing relies on motivating satisfied and delighted customers as a referral base, who can stand as reference to the company and the brand, educate consumers, and share their experience to motivate cognitive process among consumers. The referral groups also help companies toward acquiring new consumers and develop transparency in process of decision making among consumers.

Major advantages of referral marketing programs include greater credibility of experience of peers, family, and friends. This program enhances outreach of consumers to brands, products, and services, and develops a sustainable convergence among need-product-service through fair cognitive analytics among consumers.

The successful referral program strategies may be cited of some international companies including Dropbox, Roku, PayPal, Digitalis, and Omaha Steaks, where consumers get attracted to the products and services upon learning from fellow consumers who serve as referrals (Berman 2016).

Family is another group, which influences the behavior of individuals including buying behavior. Two types of family may be distinguished from one another, the nuclear family and the extended family. Families often form a decision-making unit (DMU) with respect to household purchases, with each member performing a different role. Individual members of families often serve different roles in decision process. Some individuals manage information, by seeking details about products and services of relevance. These individuals often have a great deal of power, and they develop categorically the list of preferred and alternative decisions

(Kozak and Karadag 2012). However, referrals or influencers might not have the power to decide between preferred and alternative decisions. The decision maker holds the power to determine issues such as:

- Whether to buy
- Which product to buy
- Which brand to buy
- Where to buy it
- When to buy

Family decisions are often subject to a great deal of conflict, and often generate cognitive fatigue. The cognitive fatigue is operationally defined as decline in alerting, orienting, and executive attention performance. Some family members may resort to various strategies to get their way, like bargaining or trade-offs, wherein one member will give up something in return for someone else.

The main reason for making family-driven purchase decisions is the beliefs, trust, sense of security, convenience, and the justification of common needs. A trade-off with other decisions of individuals is evaluated with respect to rationale, resources, and perceived use value, to support the decisions. The head of the family remains as the most important financial contributor in the family, and has authority to approve decisions. It is important for the companies to understand the intrafamily dynamics and relationships as well, which play a significant role in the cognitive process, developing purchase intentions, and decision making (Verma and Kapoor 2003).

Endogenous Influences

Endogenous influences are internal to the individual. These are psychological in nature and include needs and motives, perceptions, learning processes, attitudes, personality type, and self-image. The endogenous factors are oriented toward needs and motivations, which are often viewed to be interchangeable, though they are different from cognitive perspectives. When an individual recognizes a need, it acts to trigger a motivated state of mind. Need recognition occurs when the individual becomes aware of a discrepancy between his/her actual state and some perceived desired state. Neuro-scientifically, a need is a perceived difference between an ideal and desired state, which is sufficiently large and important to stimulate a behavioral reaction over time. The evidence of learning is based on a person's behavior, emerging from experiencing a particular situation. The theory of learning suggests that learning occurs with interactions between drives, stimuli, cues, responses, and reinforcements. A drive is a strong internal stimulus impelling action, whereas motivation is a stimulus to action exhibiting how a consumer perceives situations, products, promotional messages, and even the source of such messages, in order to determine appropriate actions. Most consumers choose selective attention and retention of their perceptions during the cognitive process leading to formation of attitude and behavior.

Attitudes are enduring, but may change gradually over time. The consumer attitudes are learned from the experience and perceptions drawn on using the brands, products, or services and lead an impact to drive the behavior. Attitudes reflect the predispositions of a consumer toward other products and services. A consumer may be either favorably or unfavorably predisposed toward a brand, or may not display any behavioral pattern with respect to it. Implementation of effective customer-centric strategies by the retailing firms results in developing "TIC effect" among consumers. TIC effect is comprised of three cognitive factors including trust, involvement and commitment, driving consumer behavior in a given marketplace, which are exhibited in Figure 3.2. In a retail environment, trust may be understood as a concept, which is often related to a customer's willingness to rely upon retailing a firm's services quality and customer relations. This concept represents quality in the sense that it helps to reduce uncertainty in complex consumer–retailer relationships (Bruhn 2003). Consumers' involvement with the retailing firm, store brand, and promotions develops loyalty in the end. When consumers feel satisfaction having their association with the retail brand, their sense of commitment and involvement is enhanced. Higher levels of involvement lead to greater levels of consumer loyalty and a lower need for scarce marketing resources. Hence, involvement does play a significant moderating role and in most cases, and the relationships with the retailing firms and their store brands are stronger for consumers with higher involvement

(Baker, Cronin, and Hopkins 2009). Commitment as a concept is closely associated with the customer relationship strategy where two parties lean toward loyalty, and show stability to each other. It is also observed that a high commitment level may be an important emotional barrier in switching behavior (Hulten 2007). Customer relationships with retailers are dependent upon specific cultural contexts, in which buyers and sellers interact, and the type of relationship developed over the period determines the strength of commitment (Dash, Bruning, and Guin 2009).

Five essential qualities of esthetic judgment, including *interest, subjectivity, exclusivity, thoughtfulness, and internality,* need to be nurtured among consumers to develop conviction in buying. The quality of esthetic judgment driven by in-store aura and arousal on new products, exercised by the customers in association with the sales promoters, determines the extent to which new products and brands promoted enhance quality of life (Dobson 2007). Convergence of sales promotion, customer's perceptions, value for money, and product features drive arousal among customers. The nature of customer–retailer relationship functions as the key in selling and buying processes in reference to in-store promotions. However, in this process the perceptual problems with customers can greatly devalue the customer–promoter relationship and the brand as a whole (Platz and Temponi 2007).

Stimulus–Response Convergence

The major attribute of consumer perceptions is the underlying arousal during the process of responding to societal and business stimuli in the cognitive process of consumers. In direct-to-customers communication practice, consumers are continuously blitzed with relationship calls and marketing messages including television commercials, e-mail solicitations, and business circulars of the company. However, often persuasion punches on right customers, and stimulates the buying need to elicit the desired response on the prospected product or service. It might be very difficult for salespeople to identify what drives consumer behavior, largely because there are so many possible combinations of stimuli. Although innovative marketing strategies have always been a creative endeavor toward creating consumer behavior, adopting a scientific approach to it could make the consumer experience process easier and supportive to cognitive perceptions to enhance the customer value. "Experimental perceptions" techniques, which have long been applied by some prominent direct-selling companies such as Avon International, Dell Computers, and the like, let the salespeople engender stimuli by testing just a few of behavioral designs of customers. During the process of creating consumer awareness and prompting cognitive process, consumers lean toward testing combinations of critical attributes including perceived use value, price sensitivity, prolonged guarantee, loyalty benefits, and lifetime service to gain confidence on the brands, products, and services.

There is a strong relationship between stimulus and response in the cognitive process. Such cognitive interrelationship can be explained as an approach to develop attitude and behavior that relies on the cognitive ability of consumers to deliver comprehensive knowledge on the product or service (stimulus). The purpose of the cognitive interrelationship approach is to obtain a conviction from the buyer (response) toward his possible association as indicated in Figure 3.2. A balance between the extent of stimulus and quality of response needs to be developed among consumers to support their decision-making process. Stimulus and response are the attributes of an individual, hence the information dissemination and promotional strategies should not be generalized and applied to a group of consumers. Instead, they need to be crafted case by case to optimize the quality of decisions. The stimulus–response (SR) cognitive model in the context of decision-making process may be stated as a cognitive progression of cause and effect relationship. In managing in SR course, companies need to deliver comprehensive information after identifying the needs of customers and problems, so that the cognitive abilities of consumers will flow naturally from the consumers' mindset to the object-brand, product, or service. The thinking process of consumers must be guided through the following cognitive designing process:

- Stimulus–response analysis
- Mind mapping of consumers
- Problem-need-solution nexus
- Maximizing consumer satisfaction

Many psychological experiments have shown that subjects respond in a predictable manner when exposed to a specific stimulus. When subjects are rewarded for correct responses, the responses may become automatic. Companies using the SR approach concentrate on saying the right thing at the right time to develop a favorable response from the prospect. Knowing how brands normally respond to certain stimuli helps consumers build a sequence of cognitive outcomes. Stimuli are derived from various interrelated factors that affect the cognitive process of a person in a given time and space. Consumer stimuli are derived from market-related point-of-sale offers and relational factors, which steer the analytics in the mindset of consumers. The opinion of fellow consumers, peers, and self-reference criterion also contribute to the information-steering process. The salespeople generally drive the factors of market stimuli during direct-selling interface. Churning of information from all available sources generates arousal, silence, or alienation among the consumers, which emerge as a response to various buying preferences. The referral customers, who play a vital role in promoting a vast array of brand information, generate peer influence.

During the cognitive process toward decision making, illustrative cognitive mapping of thoughts helps the consumers, and makes sure the prospect absorbs the context and contents of the discussion.

The effect of stimulus–response mapping among complex consumers is a difficult process. However, stimuli generated by brands might differ from self-reference stimuli acquired by the consumer during his search for products or services.

Therefore, the degree of consistency and variability of information delivery by the salespeople affect the stimulus–response quality and time of consumers. It is observed that consistent SR mapping leads to faster and more accurate initial consumer decision making on buying (Madhavan and Gonzalez 2010). Cognitive maps track the natural progression of consumer's thought process by allowing it to connect with each new thought to the ones that have come before; whereas linear notes or lists deliberately cut off each idea from the ones proceeding and following it, thereby stimulating the natural thinking process. Cognitive maps can also be used by the referral consumers in informal meetings with consumers, as a sort of visual agenda on Facebook or live chat in any electronic platform, toward delivering more lively and participatory learning process (Harvard Business School 2000).

Among various promotional offers, price discounts, free samples, bonus packs, and in-store displays are associated with product trial. Trial determines repurchase behavior and mediates in the relationship between sales promotions and repeat buying behavior (Ndubisi and Moi 2005). Repeat buying behavior of customers is largely determined by the values acquired on the product. The attributes, awareness, trial, availability, and repeat (AATAR) factors influence the customers toward making rebuying decisions in reference to the marketing strategies of the firm. The decision of customers on repeat buying is also affected by the level of satisfaction derived on the products, and the number of customers attracted toward buying the same product, as a behavioral determinant (Rajagopal 2005). With growing competition in retailing consumer products, innovative point-of-sale promotions offered by supermarkets are aimed at boosting sales and augmenting the store brand value. Purchase acceleration and product trial are found to be the two most influential variables of retail point-of-sale promotions. It has been found that there is a significant association between the four consumer promotional approaches, including coupons, price discounts, samples, and *buy-one-get-one-free*, and the compulsive buying behavior (Gilbert and Jackaria 2002). The occurrence and the choice of appropriate retail promotion techniques are important decisions for retailers. It is crucial for the retailing firms to apprehend the mechanisms involved at the consumer level regarding these sales promotions. Variables such as variety seeking, perceived financial benefit, brand loyalty, and store loyalty toward point-of-sale promotions have specific influences on the buying behavior and volume of retail sales (Laroche et al. 2003).

Customer Value and Loyalty

The customer value is an intangible factor, which has a significant role in influencing the buying decisions. The customer value broadly includes psychometric variables like brand name, loyalty, satisfaction, and referral opinions. The consumer lifetime value is built over time by the business firms, which also contributes to the individual perceptions of the customers, and augments their value. The new school of business thoughts and contemporary researchers have emphasized that, toward maximizing the lifetime value of customers, a firm must manage customer relationships for the long term. In disagreement to this notion, a study demonstrates that firm profits in competitive environments are maximized, when managers focus on the short term with respect to their customers (Villanueva et al. 2004). When salespeople construct a customer value proposition, they often simply list all the benefits their offering might deliver. However, the relative simplicity of this all-benefits approach may have a major drawback of benefit assertion; it may lead the salespeople to claim advantages for those features of their products and services that customers do not care (Anderson, Narus, and Rossum 2006). However, salespeople should consider the following strategies for enhancing the customer value:

- Enhancing customer esteem—*you be the best judge*
- Million dollar words—*satisfaction guarantee or money back*
- Unconditional guarantee
- Conditional guarantee

Time limit, warranty, usage conditions, and maintenance only

- Creating impulse—*double guarantee, dramatize statement*
- Competitive guarantee
- Keeper offer—*premium value to customers*
- Value protection guarantee—*security against frauds*

Successful multinational companies organize their customer value and satisfaction (CVS) strategies around various key activities by developing customer-focused culture, executive support to salespeople in improving the capability and competence in prospecting customers, and improving customer-listening tools. Enhancing customer value is an organizational issue where every employee, from manager to salesperson, plays his role. It has been observed that there is an increasing number of customer goods and services offered in recent years, suggesting that product-line extensions have become a favored strategy of product managers. A larger assortment, it is often argued, keeps customers loyal and allows firms to charge higher prices.

The key marketing variables such as price, brand name, and product attributes affect customers' judgment processes, and derive inference on its quality dimensions leading to customer satisfaction. An experimental study indicates that customers use price and brand name differently to judge the quality dimensions, and measure the degree of satisfaction (Brucks, Zeithaml, and Gilian 2000). The value of corporate brand endorsement across different products and product lines, and at lower levels of the brand hierarchy, also needs to be assessed as a customer value driver. Use of corporate brand endorsement, either as a name identifier or as logo, identifies the product with the company, and provides reassurance for the customer (Rajagopal and Sanchez 2004). Amidst increasing market competition, some companies have outmaneuvered by focusing through value-for-money strategies enabling consumers to economize (manufacture at low cost and make consumers spend less), and become more efficient (manufacture at the same cost for lesser margin of profit), or become more effective (manufacture more at the low cost and lean for relatively low profit). This strategy has helped low-end firms to enhance customer value competitively and lead the marketplace (Williamson and Zeng 2009).

Consumer lifetime value (CLV) is a key metric within customer relationship management. Consumer lifetime value also represents the net present value of profits coming from the individual customer, which creates a flow of transactions over time. Firms look at their investments in terms of cost per sale, rate of customer retention, and conversion of prospects. The concept of the lifetime value of a customer is well established in the theory and practice of database marketing. The lifetime value of a customer, defined to be the expected present value of the net cash flows from the firm's relationship with the customer over his or her lifetime, is often used as an upper limit on spending to acquire the customer (Pfeifer 1999). Many firms agree that their efforts should be focused on growing the lifetime value of their customers. The customers' lifetime value is constituted by three components—customers' value over time, length of customers' association, and the services offered to the customer. The satisfaction is the customer's perception of the value received in a transaction or relationship, and it helps in making repatronage decisions based on their predictions concerning the value of a future product. It may be thus stated that the customer value paradigm is contemporary, which includes many elements of the customer satisfaction paradigm and is being more widely adopted and deployed by the firms (Rust, Zeithaml, and Lemon 2004).

Customer value is nurtured through three distinct dimensions of emotions, including pleasantness, arousal, and dominance, which have been identified as major drivers for making buying decisions among consumers. Convergence of sales promotion, consumer's perceptions, value for money, and product features drive arousal among consumers. Consumer values are created toward the new products through individual perceptions, and organizational and relational competence (Rajagopal 2007). Firms need to ascertain a continuous organizational learning process with respect to the value creation chain and measure performance of the new products introduced in the market. The product attractiveness consists of product features including improved attributes, use of advanced technology, innovativeness, extended product applications, brand augmentation, perceived use value, competitive advantages, corporate image, product advertisements, and sales and services policies associated therewith. These features contribute in building sustainable consumer values toward making buying decisions on the new products (Lafferty and Goldsmith 2004). The attractiveness of new products is one of the key factors affecting the decision making of consumers, and is related to market growth and sales. The higher the positive reactions of the consumers toward the new products in view of their attractiveness, higher the growth in sales.

Distinctiveness and Consumer Behavior

Family influence on consumption is gradually decreasing in the Western hemisphere as well as in Europe and Asia, as the globalization is growing fast in these markets. Globalization and competitive market communications are driving individualism among consumers in making their preferences and buying decisions. Young consumers frequently face an agonizing experience when the family watches their consumption pattern, and corrects their consumption behavior different from the peers. While a bitter consumer power struggle peaks within the family, consumer products companies go aggressive with their strategies in the market. To avoid problems, a critical network of family members, relatives, and outsiders must focus upon facilitating family consumers through mediation, dialogue, and future role building. The healthiest transitions involve those old-versus-young struggles, in which both the family members and the business change partners should actively participate.

Consumer culture is an integrated pattern of behavior that is consistent and compatible in its components. Such behavior is not random among consumers, but firms in a marketplace moderate the consumer behavior and drive cognitive perceptions, attitudes, and behavior over time. It is a learned behavior, not biologically transmitted. It depends on market environment and referrals. Consumer behavior is driven by the motivations of firms and consumer perceptions. Accordingly, a marketing manager of an international firm is supposed to be familiar with the reference groups, social class, consumption systems, family structure and decision making, adoption and diffusion, market segmentation, and consumer behavior, in order to understand the consumer cultural in the marketplace (Adamson 1969). Global firms make the corporate culture visible to the consumers and elevate it to priority status, often by highlighting desired values and behaviors that favor consumers.

Optimal distinctiveness is a social-psychological theory explaining within-group and outside-group differences. It asserts that individuals desire to attain an optimal balance of inclusion and distinctiveness, within and between social groups and situations. The behavior of everyone needs to belong to a group, and at the same time everyone needs to be unique, is the core argument of optimal distinctiveness theory. According to optimal distinctiveness theory, individuals strive to maintain a balance between the need to be assimilated by the peers and family, and the need for autonomy and differentiation. Optimal distinctiveness is a social psychological theory toward understanding internal and external differences within a group of people or consumers. Consumers often form their groups of interest to share experiences and information about consumption practices. Hence, the distinctiveness theory explains the consumer behavior very closely. This concept asserts that individuals desire to attain an optimal balance of inclusion and distinctiveness within and between social groups and situations (Brewer 1991). The distinctiveness behavior exhibits the following traits among consumers who direct their decision on consumption:

- Conformity
- Differentiation
- Valuation
- Identity
- Commonality

Optimal distinctiveness theory explains why people join social groups and become so attached to them. According to the optimal distinctiveness model, social identities derive from a fundamental tension between two competing social needs—the need for inclusion and a countervailing need for uniqueness and individuation. People seek social inclusion to alleviate or avoid the isolation, vulnerability, or stigmatization that may arise from being highly individuated. It has been argued that sufficiently small minority groups are associated with greater membership trust, even among members otherwise unknown, because the groups are seen as optimally distinctive (Brewer 2007; Leonardelli and Loyd 2016).

Various interest groups influence consumers' cognitive process and decision-making skills. Most consumers make their purchase decisions based on peer observations, and opinions of referrals. Such consumers avoid self-directed decisions, and believe in putting them into a group for acquiring reference on the products and services they are intending to have. In addition, many consumers are experimental in nature, buy products to experience their consumption decisions, test self-concepts on use value and value for money, review technology applications, and tend to refer them to the like-minded people. Consumers largely engage in buying multiple products and services at the same time such as clothing and accessories, restaurants or club memberships, as a symbiotic decision. Such consumer decisions are commonly driven by a group of close acquaintance of a consumer such as family, known social circle, workplace members, peer community, or culture. A useful framework of analysis of group influence on the individuals may need to be done by the companies in order to find the right reference group, its members, attributes, and trends. Reference groups serve across the social networks in several different forms and with varied social goals.

Social interactions establish the roles that people play in a society and their authority/responsibility patterns. These roles and patterns are supported by society's institutional framework, which includes education and marriage. Consider the traditional marriage of an Indian woman, which is largely arranged by the parents. The social role assigned to the women is to abide to the norms of the society and culture therein, and yield to the social pressures. Hispanic consumers spend heavily on the basics, including packaged goods and wireless phone services. Companies are funneling much of their Hispanic marketing budgets into Spanish-language TV. It is critical for retailers and marketers to understand the wide range of factors driving Hispanic consumers' shopping behavior. Retailing firms explore the shopping behavior of Hispanic consumers considering their preferred buying place, buying practices, and the way retailers and marketers intend to adapt product offerings and promotions to satisfy this rapidly growing and diverse consumer segment. For Hispanic consumers, shopping is considered a family affair, an outing for all ages from grandparents to children. Retailers looking ahead to attract the attention of the Hispanic consumers create a family-friendly atmosphere, such as balloons and providing rest areas for seniors, in order to augment the shopping response. Retailing firms in the United States train salespeople in managing customer relationship distinctly with the Hispanic consumers. While respect is a fundamental of customer relations across the board, there is a certain reverence to be extended to elders within the Hispanic culture, and is observed by the sales staff in dealings with older shoppers (Rajagopal 2015).

The concept of self-reference among consumers is a relevant framework for developing effective cognitive support toward buying decisions made on a particular product. The self-reference criteria are largely governed by the social and economic factors such as social status of owning the product, value for money, and perceived use value of the product. Some studies on consumer psychology have addressed these issues in the context of sense of control, beliefs about the length of association with the products, and the management of perceived value during the pre- and postsales situations. Such experience tends to increase the loyalty for products, brands, and firms, and determines the long-term lifestyle changes. Most growing companies have the vision to consistently create or introduce new social business initiatives with customers and suppliers, and incorporate social data into their enterprise resources planning systems. Organizations intend to employ social software, social media, and social networking to improve their relationship with customers. They monitor online communities, create and support virtual communities, develop new communication channels, and foster a wide range of strategies to promote the business of the company. Such strategies include coupons, sweepstakes, contests, and other sponsored events. Consumer involvement in social networks and company's external relations helps in developing sustainable customer value. The customer value is considered an important parameter for the companies to play a defensive role in the marketplace for acquiring and retaining customers. Building up customer value, involving them in the various products and services from designing to delivery, and serviceability help the company in gaining competitive advantage. Customer value generation helps the company in improving customer value through faster response times for new products, which is a significant way to gain competitive advantage. Many approaches to new product development emerge in the globalization process, which exhibit an internal focus and view the new product development process as terminating with product launch.

Consumption is a process influenced by the sociocultural, personal, and cognitive factors that orient consumers toward use of goods and services upon making appropriate decision to buy. Consumption is at the end of the value chain of products and services, whereby the backward and forward linkages culminate in generating value to the consumers. The social, cultural, and economic values of consumption in the value chain proceed through production of goods and services to distribution within the given business ambiance. Consumer preferences for products and services are largely driven by the value for money, and individual parameters of satisfaction associated with them. Consumers evaluate their consumption in reference to the set personal and sociocultural measures that include attractiveness, competitive advantages, sustainability, and absolute and derived satisfaction. The effect of such consumption determines the resources for the next round of economic consumption (Rajagopal and Castaño 2016). Besides personal and sociocultural factors, consumer economics are also governed by the marketing mix in the competitive markets today. As innovation, technology, and market competition are growing manifold since the inception of globalization process, consumer needs have shifted rapidly.

Summary

This chapter enables learning on various perspectives of decision process among consumers through the decision theories supported by applied examples of consumer products companies. The discussion establishes a prolific learning link between market stimuli driven by the companies and their effect on streamlining the cognitive process of consumers. The critical analysis of social learning, drive, and cue theories explained by the products and services illustrations in the marketplace provides a synergetic learning opportunity on the consumer behavior aspects. This chapter helps readers learn about exogenous and endogenous factors that affect the behavior and drive the stimulus–response cognition among consumers. In addition, several factors affecting value and lifestyle, and distinctive behavior of consumers also deliver active knowledge on the cognitive perspectives of consumers in the current marketplace environment.

References

Adamson, H. 1969. *Man, Culture and Society*. New York, NY: Oxford University Press.

Anderson, J.C., J.A. Narus, and W.V. Rossum. 2006. "Customer Value Propositions in Business Markets." *Harvard Business Review* 84, no. 3, pp. 91–9.

Baker, T.L., Jr., J.J. Cronin, and C.D. Hopkins. 2009. "The Impact of Involvement on Key Service Relationships." *Journal of Services Marketing* 23, no. 2, pp. 114–2.

Bandura, A. 1977a. *Social Learning Theory*. Englewood Cliffs, NJ: Prentice-Hall.

Bandura, A. 1977b. "Self-Efficacy: Toward a Unifying Theory of Behavior Change." *Psychological Review* 84, no. 2, pp. 191–215.

Bandura, A. 1985. "Observational Learning." In *Advances in Social Learning Theory*, ed. S. Sukemune. Tokyo, Japan: Kaneko-shoho.

Berman, B. 2016. "Referral Marketing: Harnessing the Power of Your Customers." *Business Horizons* 59, no. 1, pp. 19–28.

Booth, D.A., and R.P.J. Freeman. 2014. "Mind Reading Versus Neuromarketing: How Does a Product Make an Impact on the Consumer?" *Journal of Consumer Marketing* 31, no. 3, pp. 177–89.

Brewer, M. 1991. "The Social Self: On Being the Same and Being Different at the Same Time." *Personality and Social Psychology Bulletin* 17, no. 5, pp. 475–82.

Brewer, M. 2007. "Optimal Distinctiveness Theory." In *Encyclopedia of Social Psychology*, eds. R.F. Baumeister and K.D. Vohs, 638–9. Thousand Oaks, CA: Sage.

Brucks, M., V.A. Zeithaml, and N. Gilian. 2000. "Price and Brand Name as Indicators of Quality Dimensions of Customer Durables." *Journal of Academy of Marketing Science* 28, no. 3, pp. 359–74.

Bruhn, M. 2003. *Relationship Marketing: Management of Customer Relationships.* Harlow, UK: Pearson Education.

Dash, S., E. Bruning, and K.K. Guin. 2009. "A Cross-Cultural Comparison of Individualism's Moderating Effect on Bonding and Commitment in Banking Relationships." *Marketing Intelligence & Planning* 27, no. 1, pp. 146–69.

Dobson, J. 2007. "Aesthetics as a Foundation for Business Activity." *Journal of Business Ethics* 72, no. 1, pp. 41–6.

Dutra, A., J. Frary, and R. Wise. 2004. "Higher-Order Needs Drive New Growth in Mature Consumer Markets." *Journal of Business Strategy* 25, no. 5, pp. 26–34.

Gilbert, D.C., and N. Jackaria. 2002. "The Efficacy of Sales Promotions in UK Supermarkets: A Consumer View." *International Journal of Retail & Distribution Management* 30, no. 6, pp. 315–22.

Greenyer, A. 2008. "Are We Paying Attention?" *International Journal of Bank Marketing* 26, no. 3, pp. 200–7.

Harvard Business School. 2000. "Mind Mapping." *Harvard Business Publishing Newsletter* November, 01.

Hulten, B. 2007. "Customer Segmentation: The Concepts of Trust, Commitment and Relationship." *Journal of Targeting, Measurement and Analysis for Marketing* 15, no. 4, pp. 256–69.

Joyce, B.R., and M. Weil. 2004. *Modes of Teaching*, 4th ed. Boston, MA: Pearson.

Kapoor, A., and C. Kulshrestha. 2009. "Consumers' Perceptions: An Analytical Study of Influence of Consumer Emotions and Response." *Direct Marketing: An International Journal* 3, no. 1, pp. 186–202.

Kozak, M., and L. Karadag. 2012. "Who Influences Aspects of Family Decision-Making?" *International Journal of Culture, Tourism and Hospitality Research* 6, no. 1, pp. 8–20.

Lafferty, B.A., and R.E. Goldsmith. 2004. "How Influential are Corporate Credibility and Endorser Attractiveness When Innovators React to Advertisement for a New High Technology Product?" *Corporate Reputation Review* 7, no. 1, pp. 24–6.

Laroche, M., F. Pons, N. Zgolli, M.C. Cervellon, and C. Kim. 2003. "A Model of Consumer Response to Two Retail Sales Promotion Techniques." *Journal of Business Research* 56, no. 7, pp. 513–22.

Leonardelli, G.J., and D.L. Loyd. 2016. "Optimal Distinctiveness Signals Membership Trust." *Personality and Social Psychology Bulletin* 42, no. 7, pp. 843–54.

Madhavan, P., and C. Gonzalez. 2010. "The Relationship Between Stimulus-Response Mappings and the Detection of Novel Stimuli in a Simulated Luggage Screening Task." *Theoretical Issues in Ergonomics Science* 11, no. 5, pp. 461–73.

McEachern, M.G., and P. McClean. 2002. "Organic Purchasing Motivations and Attitudes: Are They Ethical?" *International Journal of Consumer Studies* 26, no. 2, pp. 85–92.

Mitra, A. 2005. "Digitial Memory." *Journal of Information, Communication and Ethics in Society* 3, no. 1, pp. 3–13.

Ndubisi, N.O., and C.T. Moi. 2005. "Customers Behavioral Responses to Sales Promotion: The Role of Fear of Losing Face." *Asia Pacific Journal of Marketing and Logistics* 17, no. 1, pp. 32–49.

Paladino, A. 2005. "Understanding the Green Consumerism: An Empirical Analysis." *Journal of Customer Behaviour* 4, no. 1, pp. 69–102.

Pfeifer, P.E. 1999. "On the Use of Customer Lifetime Value as a Limit on Acquisition Spending." *Journal of Database Marketing* 7, no. 1, pp. 81–6.

Platz, L.A., and C. Temponi. 2007. "Defining the Most Desirable Outsourcing Contract Between Customer and Vendor." *Management Decision* 45, no. 10, pp. 1656–66.

Puri, S., and S. Krishna. 2016. *Puma's Challenge to Maintain Leadership in India.* Cambridge, MA: Harvard Business School Press.

Rajagopal., and R. Sanchez. 2004. "Conceptual Analysis of Brand Architecture and Relations within Product Categories." *Journal of Brand Management* 11, no. 3, pp. 233–47.

Rajagopal. 2005. "Buying Decisions Towards Organic Products: Analysis of Customer Value and Brand Drivers." *International Journal of Emerging Markets* 2, no. 3, pp. 236–51.

Rajagopal. 2007. "Stimulating Retail Sales and Upholding Consumer Value." *Journal of Retail and Leisure Property* 6, no. 2, pp. 117–35.

Rajagopal. 2008. *Brand Management: Strategy, Measurement and Yield Analysis.* Hauppauge, NY: Nova Science Publishers Inc.

Rajagopal., and R. Castano. 2015. *Understanding Consumer Behaviour and Consumption Experience.* Hershey, PA; IGI Global.

Rajagopal. 2016. *Sustainable Growth in Global Markets: Strategic Choices and Managerial Implications.* Basingstoke, Hampshire, UK: Palgrave Macmillan.

Rust, R.T., V.A. Zeithaml, and K.N. Lemon. 2004. "Customer Centered Brand Management." *Harvard Business Review* 82, no. 9, pp. 110–8.

Sharma, T.G., S. Suraj, M. Srivastava, T. Chandoke, and P. Prakash. 2017. *Netflix in India: The Way Ahead*. Cambridge, MA: Harvard Business School Press.

Simpson, P.M., J.A. Siguaw, and J.W. Cadogan. 2008. "Understanding the Consumer Propensity to Observe." *European Journal of Marketing* 42, no. 1, pp. 196–221.

Verma, D.P.S., and S. Kapoor. 2003. "Dynamics of Family Decision-making: Purchase of Consumer Durables." *Paradigm* 7, no. 2, pp. 20–39.

Villanueva, J., P. Bharadwaj, Y. Chen, and S. Balasubramanian. 2004. *Managing Customer Relationships- Should Managers Really Focus on Long Term*. IESE Business School, Working Paper # D/560, May, pp. 1–37.

Williamson, P.J., and M. Zeng. 2009. "Value for Money Strategies for Recessionary Times." *Harvard Business Review* 87, no. 3, pp. 66–74.

CHAPTER 4

Behavioral Patterns and Performance Appraisal

Overview

Consumer behavior is formed by various cognitive, physiological, exogenous, and endogenous elements. Consumer-centric companies periodically map behavioral patterns of consumers by understanding major behavioral theories and interpreting them to develop appropriate strategies. Besides discussion on the shifting behavioral pattern of consumers today, this chapter discusses major personality theories encompassing big-five personality theory, psychoanalytic theory, cognitive bias, and theories of emotions. Management judgments concerning brands, products, and services have been categorically discussed in this chapter. Among applied discussions on self-governing theories, this chapter also explains equity theory and expectancy theory in reference to contemporary business environment. There are various cultural attributes like family, decision-making units (DMUs), language, religion, and esthetics, which help companies in building behavioral brands. These perspectives have also been discussed in this chapter in reference to consumer behavior.

Consumer Values and Behavioral Pattern

One of the principal drivers of consumer behavior is the dominance of social interactions. The involvement of consumers' products depends not only on their own perceptions but also on peers' response to their personality and change proneness. The relation between clothes and identity is perceived by the consumers from the perspective of their values generated in various social interactions. Consumers get involved in exhibiting lifestyle as an esthetic way of presenting their personality (Pinheiro 2008).

In this process, there are both cognitive and affective incentives that translate into potential welfare gains (or indifference) for the consumer in a given social and work-related environment. Customer preference and value placed on designer apparel are largely influenced by the social differentiation of products and self-esteem of the consumer (Moon, Chadee, and Tikoo 2008). These attributes are likely to vary depending on the customers' cultural orientation. The cultural dimensions of individualism, uncertainty avoidance, power distance, and masculinity should be a useful framework to explain cross-cultural differences in customer acceptance of designer products. Fashion products are often used for their symbolic value reflecting the personality and status of the user. When the apparel holds a designer brand, it may be perceived as an ostentatious display of wealth. Thus, consumers are motivated by a desire to impress others with their ability to pay particularity high prices for prestigious products (Solomon 1983). Such personality dimensions often play a critical role in shifting the consumer culture toward brand-led buying behavior of utilitarian goods.

Companies need to understand the factors that drive consumer stimuli toward getting associated with new products and brands. The cognitive drivers that affect consumer behavior are given as follows:

- Social status to acquire and use specific products
- Self-esteem and personality enhancement
- To make contribution to the society and business by service as lead user and brand ambassador
- To satisfy hedonic value and self-governance
- To stay in public domain and gain social prominence by getting involved in the green products and with eco-friendly companies

The role of customer value has been largely recognized over time by the firms as an instrument toward stimulating market share and profit optimization. The customer values for a new product of a firm in competitive markets are shaped more by habits, reinforcement effects, and situational influences than strongly held attitudes. The customer value is an intangible factor, which has a significant role in influencing the buying decisions.

The customer value broadly includes psychometric variables like brand name, loyalty, satisfaction, and referral opinions. The consumer lifetime value is built over time by the business firms, which also contributes to the individual perceptions of the customers and augments their value.

Most consumer products tend to enhance customer value by employing behavioral promotion strategies including personality, image, reputation and trust (PIRT). The concepts of image and reputation have been increasingly emphasized through consumer relations and value driven promotion strategies. It is argued that consumer creativity, interactions with the consumer communities, and brand-specific emotions and attitudes. PIRT attributes drive not only the brand passion among consumers but also develop attitude towards repeat buying. Companies focus on understanding differentials in consumer personality traits and strategically develop favorable PIRT attributes. Accordingly, perceived attractiveness of consumer benefits by bridging the gaps between expectations and consumer value delivery and foster consumer-corporate association.

The modern market has emerged with the announcement that ethnic dressing comes from the core of the traditional culture, whose gorgeous fabrics have been facelifted as convenience apparel within societal value and lifestyle (VALS) system. It is argued that shifts in consumer culture provide a stimulus to dynamic innovation in the arena of personal taste and consumption. Such dynamism in consumer preferences is considered as part of an international cultural system, and is driven by continuous change in VALS. The consumer values like functionality, fitness for purpose, and efficiency significantly contribute in driving cultural change and recognizing suitable lifestyles (Hartley and Montgomery 2009).

Emotions play an important role in consumer personality and so in decision making. The influence of consumer emotions and perceptions is complex, as they often turn subtle, rather than intense. Emotional reactions are often more persuasive, and short-lived emotions can have lasting effects on their personality and abilities to make decisions. The experience and expression of emotions are often sustainable, reactive, and remembered by the consumers for decision making. Understanding consumer emotions can help managers tailor their strategies to give better prompts to deliver desired responses in order to maximize customer satisfaction and loyalty (Andrade and Capizzani 2011). In order to portray consumer personality, companies need to observe the cognitive process of consumer choice, beliefs, trust, perceptions, attitude, and behavior carefully, and map their decision touchpoints. Consumers of a particular company within a brand family experience the similar decision touchpoints and values. Accordingly, companies can understand emotions, rationale, and values of consumers associated with the brands, and develop a cross-functional strategic tool that builds the desired consumer personality (Rosenbaum, Otalora, and Ramirez 2017).

Personality Theories

Exploring personalities and discovering the complexities of human behavior have always been critical to psychology excerpts over centuries. Human personality has often been discovered in two facets—exogenous and endogenous. The human personality, which is developed with the influence of external factors like family, society, acquired culture, corporate and social communications, and political stimuli, is exogenous. On the contrary, endogenous personality is based on self-reference and inner orientation of a person. Endogenous personality exhibits largely self-driven, unipolar, and depressed attributes. However, some people with endogenous attributes also show bipolar tendencies with aggressive and unpredictable behavior. Consumers with exogenous personality are open to new products and services experiments, responsive to the brand promotions and corporate communications, and interactive to the digital network, unlike consumers with endogenous personality.

The relationship between brand personality and consumer personality is symbiotic in the marketplace. Consumer-centric companies engage in conversation with consumers to understand their personality attributes and build brand personality in line with consumers' own personality traits. Individual and brand personality has significant impact on brand preference for the considered brand by the consumers. This implies that, at the time of brand preference, consumers give due importance to individual traits and brand personality. A strong and clear brand personality indicates an appropriate match with the consumer personality, which influences consumer preferences at the time of buying decision (Banerjee 2016). Customers choose a particular product or service because it expresses their personality or social status, or to satisfy particular psychological needs. Personality traits interact with customer responses on sharing experiences and create a particular attitude about the organization. Such personality traits might lead to attitudinal intentions and subsequent behaviors. Among varied perspectives of personality, one comprehensive definition introduced by Carver and Scheier (2004) characterizes personality as a dynamic, internal organization of psychological systems, which creates a person's attributes of behaviors, thoughts, and feelings. This argument stresses the psychological as well as behavioral aspects of personality traits, shows how a person might relate to the world, and reflects personality in different behaviors, thoughts, and feelings (Al-hawari 2015).

Personality traits embed consumer motivations, preferences, and desired value. The development of insight into the effect of customers' personality traits on ensuing consumer engagement can help managers make better segmentation decisions. It can also help managers achieve excellence by modifying brand communities in accordance with consumers' specific personality-based traits. Building brand personality congruent to consumer personality traits would help generating high customer loyalty to focal brands. Therefore, it can be argued that personality is a highly relevant factor in determining consumer behavior on choices, and buying decisions. It is important to identify consumers' specific personality traits that facilitate their engagement with brands and buying decisions (Hollebeek, Glynn, and Brodie 2014; Islam, Rahman, and Hollebeek 2017). The brand personality provides depth, feelings, and liking to the relationship. Major consumer personalities are discussed in Table 4.1.

The brand personality has product attributes, corporate image, and brand attributes, resulting from the other two variables. The customer needs, perceived use value associated with the product, and the attitudinal variables of the customer form the core of customer personality as exhibited in Table 4.1. The relationship between the brand and customer personalities has three dimensions—strong, vacillating, and weak. The strong hold of the customer relationship with brands leads to loyalty development while the weak links form the discrete relationship. The

Table 4.1 Major perspectives in consumer personality and marketer's approach

Perspectives	Major concepts	Marketer's approach
Biological	Temperament, evolution, adaptation, altruism, sexual jealousy, heredity, neurotransmitter pathways, and cerebral hemisphere function	Consumer-centric companies track consumer temperament like happiness, anger, confusion, and sadness over their brands. Companies try to develop next-generation brands observing the consumer behavior. Most companies continuously provide stimuli to consumers and prompt their response. Such practices drive dynamic consumer behavior.
Cognitive	Expectancy, self-efficacy, outcome expectation, schema, personality variables, personality construct, reciprocal determinism, modeling, constructive choices, life-narratives, and perceptual maps	Most consumers possess variety-seeking behavior, and their preferences and expectancy levels keep changing. Cognitive dynamics of consumers are complex and require exogenous and endogenous support. Therefore, consumer-oriented companies not only invest in educating consumers but also ensure positive self-reference, and encourage feedback from consumer communities.
Humanistic	Self-actualization, creativity, flow, spirituality, personal responsibility, freedom, choice, openness to experience, unconditional positive regard, acceptance, empathy, real self, hierarchy of needs, peak experience, and positive psychology	Most consumer products companies cocreate products in order to generate positive perceptions, real-self, preferred choice, and empathy among consumers. To drive self-actualization and self-esteem among consumers, companies introduce innovative and high-quality products. Social and cultural stimuli are also strategically planned by the companies to drive self-esteem of consumers.
Learning	Reinforcement, punishment, stimulus, response, conditioning, extinction, shaping, discrimination learning, generalization, situation, act frequency, basic behavioral repertoire, labeling, gradients of approach, and avoidance	Most companies succeed in the consumer markets through trial-and-error strategies. However, the most significant step in this process is to know the problems and develop a right solution. Reinforcing, conditioning, shaping, delivering new communication to consumers, and ratifying failure brands, products, and services are commonly followed by the companies to create or revive consumer perceptions, attitude, and behavior.

| Traits | Extraversion (talkative, assertive, energetic), agreeableness (good-natured, cooperative, trustful), conscientiousness (orderly, responsible, dependable), neuroticism (calm, non-neurotic, sustainable), and culture (intellectual, polished, independent-minded) | Consumer personality traits helps companies to develop cognitive stimuli and motivation among consumers in order to make positive perceptions, attitude, and behavior toward brands, products, and services. Companies should understand consumer traits meticulously. Research on consumer behavior reveals new dimensions on change in preferences and perceptions among consumers. |

vacillating dimension cultivates the risk of brand switching due to uncertainty of consumer decision to get associated with the brand or otherwise. The cognition and emotion form a complex and inseparable relationship within higher-order human cognitive behavior. High-resolution images, nonverbal illustrations, and videos drive emotions among consumers and develop cognitive affinity, biasness, or defecation, which intervene in their personality and decision-making process. In the context of consumer behavior, emotions play a substantial role in understanding features of brands, products, and services. From this perspective, understanding the process of the advertisements and brand communications as the base to form brand knowledge needs to be considered as a higher-order cognitive process.

Big-Five Personality Theory

Various theoretical perspectives describe personality at numerous levels of abstraction or breadth. These levels have made unique contributions over time toward understanding individual differences in behavior and experience. However, the number of personality traits, and scales designed to measure them, escalated beyond the assumptions set by the psychology thinkers and management experts during the past (Goldberg 1971; McAdams 1995). Consumers often anthropomorphize brands by endowing them with personality traits, and marketers often create or reinforce these perceptions by their brand positioning. Brand personality traits provide symbolic meaning or emotional value that can contribute to consumers' brand preferences and can be more enduring than functional attributes. Successfully positioning a brand's personality within a product category requires measurement models that are able to disentangle a brand's unique personality traits from the traits common to all brands in the product category. Consumers perceive the brand on dimensions that typically capture a person's personality, and extend that to the domain of brands. The dimensions of brand personality are defined by extending the dimensions of human personality to the domain of brands. One way to conceptualize and measure human personality is the trait approach, which states that personality is a set of traits (Anderson and Robin 1986). A personality trait is defined as any distinguishable attitude relatively enduring, in which an individual differs from others (Guilford 1973). Human personality traits are determined by multidimensional factors like the individual's behavior, appearance, attitude and beliefs, and demographic characteristics.

Consumer personality is often formed with subjective experience, self-appraisals, and individualism. External stimuli have not always been an important input in developing personalities. Self-reflection is an implicit basis for constituting personality, which largely emerges from the experience for individuals, or for consumers in general. It is explicit that the basis of personality describes life stories or narratives as important aspects of identity and functioning, which emphasize self-concept and identity (McAdams 1996). The theoretical concept of possible self-orientation demonstrates the power of self-reflective cognition to human behavior, and its need for modifications in reference to exogenous stimuli. Self-referred cognitions are obviously developed with experience, and so these concepts provide a place to link the influence of society, family, and culture on personality. The personality of an individual is not a permanent state of life, as it tends to evolve and adapt to the exogenous factors over time. Idiographic studies (psycho-historical) suggest that people keep understanding external intervention continuously and develop insights to behavior modification over time, which alter their personalities (Bornstein 2005). Therefore, consumers do not exhibit a consistent personality in consumption, and seek to modify their behavior according to the prevailing trend. Such a phenomenon in personality variations demands innovations, improvement in quality of products and services, introduction of new attributes, brand promotions, sales stimuli, and endorsements through word of mouth interpersonally, and on digital platforms.

After decades of research in exploring personality traits, the "Big Five" personality dimensions serve an integrative function in a common framework. Based on the trait theory, researchers have concluded that there are five stable personality dimensions, also called the "Big Five" human personality dimensions. From the perspective of human psychology, the personality traits are labeled by Norman (1963) as extraversion (talkative, assertive, energetic), agreeableness (good-natured, cooperative, trustful), conscientiousness (orderly, responsible, dependable), neuroticism (calm, non-neurotic, sustainable), and culture (intellectual, polished, independent-minded). However, from the consumers' perspective, in the context of business, the common personality traits are identified as described in the following:

- *Extraversion* is sometimes explained as overreaction. The broad dimension of extraversion encompasses specific traits of consumers being talkative and exhibiting active participation in digital and interpersonal platforms. Such consumers take lead in spreading the word of mouth among peers and in the society. Consumers with extroversive personality are energetic as well as assertive. Most companies use such consumers as gatekeepers, bloggers, and experiential marketers.
- *Agreeableness* is human personality, which includes the attributes of being sympathetic, kind, and affectionate. Consumers holding such personality develop self-congruence to brand attributes, and adjustable perceived value to the brands, products, and services, as they tend to compromise with the brands marginally. Consumers with agreeableness personality understand the problems of the manufacturer and the marketer, and stay sympathetic and suggestive as well. Such consumers also lean toward imparting their help in educating other consumers and guiding them toward gaining the best value of the products and services.
- *Conscientiousness* is another major factor of personality exhibited in the people as being high in conscientiousness,

organized, thorough, and planned in activity management. The level of expectation of consumers having such personality is very high from the companies. They meticulously manage their needs, desire, values, and expectations. Conscientious consumers are noncompromising and exhibit rationale, articulation, and strategy in their dealings. The quality of customer relations, brand deliverables, and brand equity matter a lot to them. Most consumer products companies develop their marketing strategies around such consumer personalities to stay ethical, premier, and competitive in the marketplace. Companies learn from such consumer personalities to build sustainable consumer touchpoints, and remain focused on consumers in the marketplace.

- *Neuroticism* is related with management of emotions, and demonstrates emotional balance. Neuroticism is characterized by traits like tense, moody, and anxious. Consumers with neurotic personality are unpredictable, bipolar, and often indecisive. Such consumers are classified as hard consumers and are found not always enthusiastic about the brand promotions, endorsements, and social networks. Companies should understand the personality of neurotic consumers and carefully deploy resources to activate their emotions toward positive attitude and behavior for their brands, products, and services. Investment on brands, products, and services targeting at neurotic consumers faces the risk of sunk cost, as the consumers might not respond to promotional strategies of the companies.

- *Openness to experience* may be explained as the ability of intellectual drive or imagination. This dimension exhibits wide interests, and being imaginative and insightful. This is a positive attitude of consumers showing their willingness to explore new perceptions, brand values, and enhance the socioeconomic impact of the brand.

Multinational companies develop advertising strategies within the "Big Five" human personality dimensions that include extraversion/

introversion, agreeableness, consciousness, emotional stability, and culture. Based on these human personality dimensions, some new dimensions related to brands, including sincerity, excitement, competence,
sophistication, and ruggedness in presenting a communication to show
the vigor of a product through advertisements, have also been identified (Aaker 1997). This paradigm suggests that the brand personality
influences consumers in reference to excitement, human personality, and
consumer desire.

It has been found by many researchers that consumers measure the
strategic fit of the brand in one or more dimensions of the aforementioned
personality traits, and make decision about further association with the
brand. The relationship between the brand and customer is largely governed by the psychographic variables that can be measured broadly by
the closeness and farness of the personalities of brand and customer.
The type of relationship that customers possess with the brands based
on the loyalty levels is an extremely significant parameter for the marketers. New-generation marketing approaches include customer-focused,
market-driven, outside-in, one-to-one marketing, data-driven marketing,
relationship marketing, integrated marketing, and integrated marketing
communications. These marketing approaches emphasize two-way communication through better listening to customers, and through the idea
that communication before, during, and after transactions can build or
destroy important brand relationships (Duncan and Moriarty 1998).

Psychoanalytic Theory

Psychoanalytic theory encompasses the human perspectives of personality
organization, and the dynamics of personality development that guide
psychoanalysis, a clinical method for treating psychopathology. Sigmund
Freud has first laid out this theory in the late 19th century focusing largely
on the human physiological needs like hunger and sex, and their impact
on behavior and personality. The psychoanalytic theory has undergone
many refinements since his work on this subject. Bowlby (1982) created
a *behavioral systems* model of motivation, in context to ethology and
cybernetic control theory. According to this theory, human behavior is
an organized and guided innate behavioral systems. This theory argues

that it develops attachments, caregiving, exploration of desire, and sexual systems, all of which facilitate the satisfaction of fundamental human needs and thereby increase the likelihood of survival and adjustment to environment.

Interpreting the psychoanalytic theories and behavioral systems from the perspective of consumers, it may be argued that a learned behavior drives a person toward predetermined goals by monitoring, appraising, and evaluating goal-relevant internal and external cues, and by learning new means-end associations. The positive stimulus-response behavior increases the likelihood of goal attainment, and facilitates need satisfaction. Hence, most consumers follow the guided path of marketers, and respond to the given stimuli, to gain desired satisfaction. However, there also exist risks in experiencing perceived values by the consumers to support behavioral outcomes. Consumer-centric companies should therefore work toward understanding the predetermined goals of consumers and create stimuli that could help in attaining higher satisfaction. The common stimuli that drive the predetermined goals of consumers include product attributes, uniqueness, perceived use value, product lifecycle, value for money, promotions, and societal image. Companies should be able to explore the consumer desires better than the apparent needs, to satisfy them with high perceived value. Exploring consumer desires would give an opportunity to the companies to identify latent demands, and gain near-monopolistic advantages upon exploiting such business situations.

Psychoanalysis opens a variety of platforms from conventional psychological theory into understanding contemporary consumption and consumerism. The psychoanalytic theory of defense and the unconscious mind provides vision on why commodities, from luxury cars to high-value gourmet chocolates, so easily substitute the common products for satisfying deeper repressed (subconscious) desires (Gabriel 2015). Understanding and reacting to the social fantasies of consumers, which are subtle in their mind like driving a sports car or experiencing zero gravity in a long-haul flight, might give the companies opportunities to serve the consumers with products and services that could offer real or pseudo satisfaction to their hidden desires. Most companies launch unique brand campaigns to bring consumers' personal and social fantasies alive, and drive impulse for consumption (Japhy 2015).

Consumer psychoanalytic theory can be understood from different perspectives in the eastern hemisphere in reference to oriental philosophies like Buddhism, Hinduism, and Confucianism. The Buddhist consumer philosophical framework delineates the consumer cognition on nature, and processes toward judging consumer mind in reference to expectations, preferences, and satisfaction. In this philosophy, the attachment to objects holds the perceptions on ownership, materialism, and excessive behaviors. The process of decision making, evaluating options, and regulating consumer mind toward marketplace morality, cognitive biases, value-based choices, and free will are governed in view of the latent desires, needs, social responsibility, self-efficacy, and cultural drivers. Thus, consumer psychology has been overly reliant on a small set of sociocultural and religious paradigms over the self-psychoanalytic variables. As a result, cognitive behavior of consumers appears fragmented toward contributing new knowledge on, and relief from, our hyper-consumption era (Mick 2017).

Theories of Emotion

Emotion is a complex psychophysiological experience among people causing perceptions, feelings, cognitive push, and arousal that drive physiological changes. Consumers in marketplace analyze information, perceive products and services, gain experience, and build arousal, which leads to a touch-feel-and-pick chain physiological action. There are positive emotions and negative emotions related to an object, an event, social emotions, self-appraisal emotions, or peer observations. Some emotions are innate, while some are acquired and shared. Satisfaction to a desire is innate emotion, while acquired emotions have exogenous influence and create a *me-too* feeling on products or services. However, some emotions are bidimensional that are innate and acquired as well. For example, products symbolizing love, care, joy, and surprise possess bidimensional emotions encompassing innate and acquired types. People share emotions of anger and fear with others to gain support and sympathy. These are known as primary emotions. Secondary emotions are those that people learn through self-actualization like pride, rage, shame, neglect, distress, sympathy, and horror. Most companies develop brand campaigns accordingly, close to emotions so that consumers can build cognitive association, perceptions, attitude, and behavior toward brands over time.

Emotional brands not only create emotional campaigns but also forge meaningful and valuable emotional connections at every touchpoint. However, brand campaigns should be consistent with the emotions they elicit and ensure consumer value and loyalty in the long run. While creating emotions through brand campaigns, companies develop complete alignment with consumer personality, to elicit and describe how brands can create and foster desires, emotions, and perceived values across all platforms, touchpoints, and consumer associations. In order to create consistency in consumer emotions, companies engage their employees and collaborators in developing credible and authentic bonding with people through shared values, attitudes, and behaviors. Companies engaged in creating brand emotions tend to develop meaningful experience, and inculcate anthropomorphic sense among consumers. For example, products of Apple Inc. foster a sense of mystery allowing Apple users to feel a part of something big and important (self-actualization), while Coca-Cola recently changed its tagline from "Open Happiness" to "Taste the Feeling" and maintained its focus on happy images of people connecting and engaging one another, such as the bond between siblings (happiness, family, bonding, love). Another example that reveals sadness in emotions is of the advertisement produced by MetLife Hong Kong exhibiting a heartbreaking message featuring a daughter who describes all the things she loves about her dad, yet the story breaks down when she also describes all the ways he lies to her. Fear and scarcity attributes also drive fear emotions that stay on the top-of-the-mind memories of consumers. Many consumer communications of insurance companies including newspaper and magazine advertisements and television commercials could be categorized as scary, and some of them might be humorous.

Emotions and physiological changes are symbiotic. *James–Lange theory* of emotions explains that physiological changes occur when a person witnesses or gets involved in the event, which causes arousal and physiological reactions (Northoff 2008). Companies engage consumers in the do-it-yourself (DIY) events wherein they gain experience, arousal, and identify emotions upon interpreting their involvement cognitively. Therefore, electronic gaming companies like Microsoft (Xbox), Sony

(PlayStation), and Nintendo attract consumers through DIY infrastructure allowing consumers to gain and share experience for indefinite time. Test drive event organized by the automobile companies is a proven marketing strategy to acquire and retain consumers. The arousal in physiological sense creates muscular tension, heart rate increases, perspiration, dryness of the mouth, and so on. The basic premise of the theory is that physiological arousal instigates the experience of emotion. Instead of feeling an emotion and subsequent physiological response, the theory proposes that the physiological change is primary, and emotion is experienced thereafter, when the brain reacts to the information received via the physiological nervous system.

Toward the advancement on the theories of emotions, *Schechter–Singer theory* explains the two-factor interaction of emotion, which states that emotion is based on physiological arousal and cognitive label. Accordingly, when an emotion is felt, a physiological arousal occurs and the person uses the immediate environment to search for emotional cues to label the physiological arousal. Sometimes, when the brain does not know why it feels an emotion, it relies on external stimulation for cues on how to label the emotion (Nisbet 2000). In order to avoid negative labeling of emotions, consumer-centric companies integrate marketing strategies combining DIY and digital information platforms for sharing consumer experience to ensure the favorable external stimuli and cues for interpreting the emotions of consumers. This theory has further evolved with the *cognitive-mediational theory* proposed by Lazarus, which explains that the stimulus leads to a 'personal meaning' derived from both arousal and the emotion. The sound of a gunshot, for example, is interpreted as something potentially dangerous and leads to both physiological responses, like a rapid heart rate and trembling, and the subjective experience of fear. The thought-provoked emotion is often referred to as cognitive (Lazarus 1982; 1991).

Cognitive Bias

A cognitive bias refers to the systematic pattern of deviation from the standard procedure or rationality in judgment, whereby inferences about other people and situations are drawn in a convenient or an illogical manner. Individuals create their own subjective reality based on self-reference or social influence. Most consumers develop opinion on brands, products, and services based on their preconceived notions, or nonevident proposition acquired from the peers or society. Most consumer-centric companies educate consumers on brand profiles and usage of products and services through interactive personal or digital platforms in order to avoid cognitive biasness among consumers. Cognitive biases among persons develop as a tendency over time, to think in certain ways that deviate from a rational standard or an established judgment. Biasness among consumers often occurs in reference to the use value of products and services, comparative advantages, value for money judgments, and societal behavior. The decision-making bias occurs among consumers also due to ambiguity inculcating the tendency to avoid options.

The cognitive bias triggers in consumers also due to the variety-seeking behavior, as too many options cloud the decision process. Accordingly, multiple perceptions drive recurring thoughts, and affect the objective-oriented decision process. Most consumer products companies optimize their product line with highly preferred products, as product overlap causes cannibalization of products within the product line. Cognitive biasness often affects consumers due to the personal beliefs and exogenous evaluation of the personal rationale as well. Often, consumers also face confirmation bias, which exhibits the tendency to search for rationale, interpret causes and effects, focus on perceived values, and refer and remember information in a way that confirms one's preconceptions. Consumers with confirmation bias personality listen, understand, and pay attention to all information around them, but yield to only those decisions that confirm their preconceived notions or cognitive biases. Such consumers are largely nonresponsive to corporate strategies, market attractions, and customer relations offered by the managers. They can be classified as hard consumers, who cannot be easily convinced for any new brand attributes, promotions, or competitive product attractions. Confirmation bias is also known as *myside bias,* which occurs when people evaluate evidence, generate evidence, and test their propositions in a manner biased toward their own prior opinions and attitudes. Research across a wide variety of myside bias paradigms reveals a somewhat surprising finding regarding individual differences.

The magnitude of the myside bias shows very little relation to intelligence (Stanovich, West, and Toplak 2013).

Consumers also suffer from outcome or judgmental bias, which illustrates the tendency to judge a decision by its eventual outcome, instead of based on the quality of the decision. Such personality biases among consumers are out of bounds of organizational and managerial strategy. However, there is also the postpurchase rationalization in terms of an eventual comprise, which exhibits the behavior of consumers to persuade oneself through rational argument that a purchase was of good value, despite the identified flaws. However, consumers who develop negative postpurchase rationale do not stay loyal to the brands. If managers are influenced by the outcomes achieved by their employees in judging the consumer behavior ethically, it can lead to *success breeds acceptance* culture. On the contrary, when organizations place undue emphasis on outcomes at the cost of standards, consumer behavior could be condoned or justified, which might jeopardize the business performance of the organization (Cardy and Selvarajan 2006).

Consumers are often biased with social status, and thus compromise with high price-high value products, even though such products might not be a necessity for them. In psychology and behavioral economics, the endowment effect, known as *divestiture aversion,* and related to the mere ownership effect in social psychology, is the hypothesis that people attribute more value to things merely because they own them or they are willing to acquire. It has been observed that people with such personality bias place a higher value on objects they own relative to the objects they do not. In an experiment, people demanded a higher price for a coffee mug that had been given to them, but put a lower price on one they did not own yet. Under the endowment effect, people often demand much more to sell an object, than they would be willing to pay to buy it (Martinez, Zeelenberg, and Rijsman 2011).

Managerial Judgments

It is argued that consumer creativity, identification with the brand community, and brand-specific emotions and attitudes including personality, image, reputation, and trust (PIRT) attributes drive the brand passion among consumers. In this process, brand knowledge is also considered as an important determinant of consumers' willingness to share their knowledge with the fellow consumers and firms (Füller, Matzler, and Hoppe 2008). Corporate factors of brand personality develop interrelationship between personality (P) and trust (T) in reference to brand image (I) and corporate reputation (R). Trust on brand is considered a key aspect of brand relationships, brand personality, and brand equity. Accordingly, PT dimensions at marketing level comprise functional, emotional, and symbolic brand benefits, while IR dimensions include corporate activities, corporate associations, organizational values, and corporate personality. Corporate values, corporate brand personality, and functional consumer benefits are the most critical and consistent predictors of both attitudinal and behavioral loyalty (Anisimova 2007). Previous researches have established that there is a close relationship between the brand attributes and the corporate brand image concerning the emotional values. This relationship in turn influences the consumer's responses toward building brand loyalty.

Perceived attractiveness of products, firms, and retail stores significantly influences the consumer-brand relationship development process in meaningful and predictable ways. Owning a brand by consumers influences their opinion of the desirability of the brand as a relationship partner. The quality connection between personality traits and brand association depends on the perceived attractiveness of the brand to a large extent. However, the role of attractiveness in the relationship varies across individual brand personality dimensions (Hayes et al. 2006). There is a significant positive relationship between brand trust and brand share in the competitive marketplace. It is also observed that the relationship between brand strength, which is determined as the degree of behavioral relevance of the brand, and brand trust catalyzes the consumer association with brands in the long run (Burmann, Zeplin, and Riley 2009). Consumer perceptions also determine the brand personality of virtual brands. Electronic retailing is primarily a functional activity, with preeminent roles for interactivity, web atmospherics, and navigability. However, users' perceptions of functional attributes are rooted in emotional associations, such as excitement or authenticity. Emotional brand associations can be utilized by e-retailers as the benchmarks of key performance indicators to improve the brand performance (Merrilees and Miller 2005).

Advertising effectiveness can be measured by brand and advertising evaluations. Effective brand management encompassing brand personality is of paramount importance in reaching the overall company goals toward satisfaction, loyalty, and profitability. Companies may choose to deliver advertising in a more appealing dimension for quick cognitive reflexes of consumers (Rajagopal 2007). It is also argued that self-image, and brand identity congruence, may be related to satisfaction in general among consumers, and it affects satisfaction of consumers and brand value of the products or firms at varied levels of expectation. In the long run such congruence can significantly influence brand preference, brand satisfaction, and purchase intentions of consumers (Jamal and Al-Marri 2008). Findings of some research studies indicate that both the affective and cognitive components of corporate brand identity drive significant influence on consumer attitudes toward the brand use, which in turn leads to more positive company attitudes and purchase intentions among consumers. The three forces that influence brand identity and consumer association consist of represented group identity, targeted brand positioning, and reconciled self-image (Jun, Cho, and Kwon 2008).

Cultural dimensions of buyers' self-image offer deeper insights regarding motives and desires on buying brands. The interaction between consumer self-image and perceived brand image moderates the decision of buyers to develop temporal association (short or long run) with the brand (Andronikidis 2008). To build and maintain consumer loyalty, brand managers supplement mass-media advertising with interactive strategies, Internet communications, and other innovative channels of distribution. However, brand managers have to face more threats to their brands, especially parity responses from competitors. Brand loyalty can yield significant marketing advantages including reduced marketing costs and greater trade leverage (Aaker 1991). The factors of human personality convey different meanings when attributed to different brands. While the psycholexical approach remains a suitable procedure to identify brand descriptors, the factors used to describe human personalities appear to be inappropriate for describing the brands studied here (Caprara, Barbaranelli, and Guido 2001; Roodenburg 2003). Extension of the psycholexical hypothesis for describing human personality serves as a metaphor to describe stable characteristics identifying brands and products. The psycholexical hypothesis is generally defined by two postulates. The first postulate states that the personality characteristics that are important to a group of people eventually become a part of that group's language. The second postulate states that more important personality characteristics are more likely to be encoded into language as a single word. These postulates also guide companies to develop an appropriate brand language (advertising contents, illustrations, and punch line), brand etymology (meaning or brand phrase), and cultural values. Attitudes toward brands probably rely on beliefs associated with a set of attributed characteristics, which make them distinctive from their competitors.

The consumer behavior emerging out of external or internal forces may be referred as derived varied behavior. Direct varied behavior has been defined in reference to "novelty," "unexpectedness," "change," and "complexity" as they are pursued to gain inherent satisfaction. In a study, the influence of product category and level attributes were examined, and six influential factors, involvement, purchase frequency, perceived brand difference, hedonic feature, strength of preference, and purchase history, have been identified (Trijp et al. 1996). Personality factors of the brands give consumers the means whereby they can make choices and judgments. Based on these experiences, consumers rely on chosen brands and sense guarantee standards of quality and service, which augments the consumer trust and brand value.

Self-Governing Theories

The major self-governing theories in social psychology refer to equity, existence, relatedness, growth, and expectancy theories. Consumer behavior is also affected by the attributes described in reference to the self-governing maxims. The core of the *equity theory* is the principle concerning the convergence of self- and societal balance or equity, which governs the behavior in general. The cognitive motivation theory argues that an individual's motivation level is correlated to his perception of equity, fairness, and justice practiced by the society. Rising inequalities and high levels of consumption in many capitalist economies can be understood as the relationship between satisfaction and consumption (Dwyer 2009). Higher the individual's perception of fairness, greater is the motivation level and vice versa. Consumer behavior is affected by the unequal consumption propensity, purchasing power, differentiation in brands, products, and services, and value propositions in the business and society. Such incidences are common, which cause behavioral discrimination, and split the societal values among consumers. Consequently, mass consumers are always found attracted toward the premium brands, and incubate latent demand over time. They wait for the opportunities to acquire premium products and get satisfied over the social inequality concerns.

Though there are consumption inequalities among consumers, there also exist some commonalities among consumers. Advancements of information technology and continuous innovations in consumer products have brought commonalities among the consumption behavior. Consumption of consumer electronics today has developed commonality among consumers. The emergence of global markets for standardized consumer products has grown to the magnitude of economies of scale. Technology, by proletarianizing (developing uniformity in perceptions, attitude, and behavior within a social class), communication, transport, and travel drives the world toward a converging commonality. Most companies have moved from emphasis on customizing items to offering globally standardized products that are advanced, functional, reliable, and low priced. They benefit from enormous economies of scale in production, distribution, marketing, and management, and engage consumers toward common consumptions (Levitt 1983). Consumption commonality is also being encouraged today by companies creating consumption communities to develop uniformity in the consumer preferences and values. Consumption communities are the groups of people who share the consumption of a brand or product. Thus, users of Apple company's products (iPhone, iPod, iPad, and Apple Watch) form a consumption community, and share common problems and success on the products and services. The consumption community perspective has also grown over the concerns of existence, relatedness, and growth concepts of individuals in the society. The consumption concerns across the socioeconomic categories of consumers are rationalized according to the following attributes of consumers:

- Safety and physical comforts
- Social needs, social relationship, and social identity
- Sense of wholeness, achievement, and fulfillment

Improving the consumption performance of consumers has been the focus of many motivation theories, especially the need theories. These theories have been questioned because of the lack of sustainable relationship between need satisfaction and product performance. Convergence of need, satisfaction, product performance, and minimizing personality differences among people has been the major challenge for several consumer products companies. Consumer communities help companies in understanding such complex behavioral convergence. The self-esteem as a personality variable exerts a significant influence on the need performance of both consumers and frontline employees of a consumer-centric company. The influence of need satisfaction, as suggested in the *existence, relatedness, and growth theory* on self-esteem (the personality trait), and the influence of self-esteem leading to performance govern the consumption culture and behavior to a large extent (Arnolds and Boshoff 2002).

Consumer expectancy is the belief that increased quality will lead to increased performance and satisfaction. The *expectancy theory* of motivation in psychology assumes that a person's behavior, which results from conscious choices among alternatives, aims at maximizing pleasure with minimum pain. Vroom (1964), realized that an employee's performance is based on individual factors such as personality, skills, knowledge, experience, and abilities. The author stated that effort, performance, and motivation are linked in a person's motivation. Therefore, most consumer-centric companies develop their product line, rationally understanding the consumer preferences and the embedded values of each preference. When the choices of consumers match with the expected value, they attain maximum satisfaction. A rational expansion of product line of the companies not only widens the scope of consumer choice but also offers value additions to the products and augments the perceived use value. Consumer expectancy encompasses the following attributes:

- Valence: the value of the perceived outcome. (What is there in the choice for me?)

- Instrumentality: the belief that if one can complete certain actions can achieve the outcome. (Is there a clear path to satisfaction?)
- Expectancy: the belief that a person is able to complete the actions. (Do I have the capability to work with choices to attain desired satisfaction by minimizing the risk?)

Expectancy can be defined as the subjective probability (because individuals differ in their estimations of the relationship between behavior and outcomes) for the individual's expectation, and as individual's anticipation about the success or failure revealing the performance (Vroom 1964; Atkinson 1957). Most consumers behave in a hedonistic way, assuming that working on best choices and preferred products would bring the highest subjective utility. Thus, most consumers fall into the cognitive bias, which drives them to realize that high-price preferences would lead to high satisfaction as against the low-price preference followed by the consumers or mass or bottom-of-the-pyramid market segments. Accordingly, the expectancy theory argues that the strength of a tendency to act in a certain way depends on the strength of an expectation that the act will be followed by a given outcome and on the attractiveness of that outcome to the individual (Robbins 1993; Suciu, Mortan, and Lazar 2013).

Cultural Attributes and Consumer Behavior

Culture may be understood as the underlying value framework that governs the individual and group behavior. It is reflected in the perceptions of individuals in observed events, in personal interactions, and in the selection of appropriate responses in social situations. Culture often manifests itself in learned behavior, as individuals grow up and gradually come to understand what their culture demands of them. Cultural attributes alter consumer behavior over time as cultural experience plays an important role in developing new perceptions and attitudes. Consumer culture is largely depicted through an ethnography-based investigation into what customers do, feel, and how they share experience. It has emerged as a powerful tool to use to gain insights into consumer behavior in a given marketplace. Most companies carryout in-depth ethnographic research and the ways to use it to their advantage. Ethnography contributes an empathic understanding of how consumers live, work, and play through gritty and detailed descriptions. Ethnographic research can pivot companies toward more meaningful attributes of consumer behavior in reference to demographics or sociocultural attributes (Cayla, Beers, and Arnould 2014).

Material culture includes the tools and artifacts (the material or physical things) in a society, excluding the physical things found in nature, unless they undergo some technological procedure. Material culture affects the level of demand, the quality, and the types of products demanded and their functional features, as well as the means of production of these goods and their distribution. Countries with large populations such as India, China, Russia, and the United States are multicultural, meaning that they contain a wide variety of cultures within their borders. Culture directly influences the consumers in reference to what they understand, analyze, and adapt. This interpretation of culture is very useful for global marketing managers. In most developing countries, family is considered as a DMU, and marital culture significantly influences perceptions, attitude, and behavior of individuals. Family is considered as a decision-making phenomenon among husbands and wives in reference to the purchase of high-involvement items. Families, as DMUs, have witnessed a tremendous shift in buying behavior in the Western countries. This is governed by demographic factors like increasing number of women in the workforce, higher educational standards, and delayed age of marriage (Gupta 2010).

Consumer brands embed emotions and personality that prompt cognitive arousal among consumers, and lead to the paradigm of perception, attitude, and formation of behavior of consumers toward brands. Consumers explore dynamic brand relationships between brand love and cocreation, and analyze how they affect behavioral branding and brand loyalty. Consumers often anthropomorphize brands in the context of their perceived value and their personality that marketers often create, to reinforce the attitude for developing behavioral brands. Consumer perceptions over time help companies in developing appropriate positioning of brands. *Behavioral brands* are grown by the companies under societal, family, and peer influence, which would moderate consumer perceptions and use values on the brands. A consumer acquires knowledge and experience on behavioral brands largely through the family and peer influence. Consumer product companies develop brand constellations to reflect the collective self-image of consumers based on emotional dispositions and peer influence (Flight and Coker 2016; Kaufmann, Correia-Loureiro, and Manarioti 2016; Fan, Wu, and Mattila 2016). Behavioral brands grow cognitively encompassing individuals, family, and society over time, and establish brand personality in the competitive marketplace. For example, companies such as Apple Inc., Colgate Palmolive, Harley Davidson, and Hershey have successfully cocreated and positioned behavioral brands by converging emotions, perceived value, and brand equity in the competitive marketplace. The *self-congruence theory* supports the explanation that customers prefer brands known for personality traits that accord with their own (Valette-Florence and Barnier 2013; Ha 2016). This is the theory of self-concept, which encompasses an individual's plan, or the articulation of the self in memory, and entails a stable and a flexible cognitive dimension. The stable element of the self-concept consists of personality characteristics that are relatively generalizable across situations and this is referred in the literature as the global self-concept or global self. While examining the cues relating to a product image, consumers search their preconceived information, and engage into a similar image from their own self-concept. However, to maintain self-consistency and promote self-esteem, individuals consume products that are of value and consistent with their self-reference and preconceived plans (Hogg, Cox, and Keeling 2000; Plewa and Palmer 2014).

Cognitive branding process is the basis for developing behavioral branding. It is a theory about how companies intending to build brands affect the perception of consumers on brands, and how, subsequently, the brands themselves influence the consumers' minds. Cognitive branding encompasses three dimensions of cognition: the meaning creation for the brand and its interpretation, the deployment of memory functions and patterns related to how brands as symbols can be perceived, personified, and used to communicate brand values, and how brands capture the attention of consumers through various emotional forms, including the activation of attention, developing attitude, and consequently behavior. The semiotics (a study of sign process—semiosis, etymology, and meaningful communication) of a brand in the process of building a behavioral brand also draws the attention of consumers, and drives social and cultural consequences (Thellefsen, Sørensen, and Danesi 2013).

Consumer-centric companies are creating behavioral brands through social media as power of popularity inculcates cognitive affinity and trust, and justifies decisions, being congruent with the trend (vogue). Therefore, behavioral brands are implanted in the society, which outgrows with individual preferences, and strengthens cognitively among consumers over time. Enhancing brand image, extending brand awareness, and facilitating customer engagement (Hollebeek 2011) are the most common social media objectives (Cawsey and Rowley 2016). The fast-moving cultural trends accelerated by the social web, and new sources of consumer insight, have all contributed to a new definition of developing behavioral brand planning. A customer-centric approach to social brand planning is critical to transform successfully the data and behavior gathered from social media into developing attitude and behavior among consumers, and delivering competitive advantage for the companies (Stauffere 2012).

Social institutions play a significant role in nurturing the cultural heritage, which is reflected in the individual behavior. Such institutions include family, education, and political structures. The media affects the ways in which people relate to one another, organize their activities to live in harmony with one another, teach acceptable behavior to succeeding generations, and govern themselves. The status of gender in society, the family, social classes, group behavior, age groups, and how societies define decency and civility are interpreted differently in every culture. Social institutions are a system of regulatory norms and rules of governing actions in pursuit of immediate ends in terms of their conformity with the ultimate common value system of a community. They constitute underlying norms and values making up the common value system of a society. Institutions are intimately related to and derived from the value attitudes common to members of a community. This establishes institutions as primarily moral phenomena, which leads to enforce individual decisions on all human needs including economic and business-related issues. The primary means for enforcement of norms is moral authority whereby an individual obeys the norm because that individual believes that the norm is good for its own sake. The relationship between the business and religion truly poses a self-challenge. Mary Kay Inc., an inter-national direct marketing cosmetics company, operates on the go-give philosophy (Weston 1999).

Esthetics may be described as the set of creative ideas embedded in culture concerning the sensory appeals of people toward beauty, art, and taste. Since actions or behavior can be said to have beauty beyond sensory appeal, esthetics and ethics often overlap to the degree that this impression is embodied in a moral or ethical code. A value system, which is the prioritization of the values held by an individual or a group in a society, forms the base of moral code. Such dimensions are reflected in the consumer behavior. In conservative societies in Asia, may be Japan or India, any communication or art that exposes women is not socially accepted, despite the esthetic standpoint of the critics. In some cultures, the relationships between moral and legal codes are often the same. Moral codes help drive personal conduct.

Esthetics includes the art, drama, music, folk culture, and architecture prevalent in a society, and these aspects of a society convey its concept of beauty and modes of expression. In different societies, colors have different significance across the countries. In Western societies, wedding gowns are usually white, but in Asia, white symbolizes peace or sorrow. The esthetic values of a society show in the design, styles, colors, expressions, symbols, movements, emotions, and postures valued and preferred in a particular culture. These attributes have an impact on the design and promotion of different products. In many situations, the symbolic expressions of communication have greater appeal than the actual words, and people respond accordingly. Therefore, an international businessperson must understand nonverbal cultural differences to avoid communicating the wrong message.

Summary

Various personality traits that guide marketers toward developing appropriate strategies, and influence consumers to make decisions congruent to their perceptions may be learnt comprehensively in this chapter. From the perspective of consumer-centric companies, major traits of consumer personality have been discussed in the chapter that helps managers to map needs, knowledge, emotions, achievements, and problems on a macro scale to develop right marketing strategies. The Big Five personality theory in conjunction with the psychoanalytic theory has been explained in this chapter to understand the behavior systems and growing fantasies of consumers. In addition, discussions on managerial judgment and self-governance theories encourage developing contextual learning and refining preconceived notions on consumer behavior.

References

Aaker, D. 1991. *Managing Brand Equity*. New York, NY: The Free Press.

Aaker, J.L. 1997. "Dimensions of Brand Personality." *Journal of Marketing Research* 34, no. 3, pp. 347–56.

Al-hawari, M.A. 2015. "How the Personality of Retail Bank Customers Interferes with the Relationship Between Service Quality and Loyalty." *International Journal of Bank Marketing* 33, no. 1, pp. 41–57.

Anderson, P.M., and L.G. Robin. 1986. *Marketing Communications: Advertising, Sales Promotion, Public Relations, Display and Personal Selling*. Englewood Cliffs, NJ: Prentice Hall.

Andrade, E.B., and M. Capizzani. 2011. *Emotional Cues That Work Magic on Customers*. Cambridge, MA: Harvard Business School Publication.

Andronikidis, A. 2008. "Psychographic Segmentation in the Financial Services Context: A Theoretical Framework." *The Marketing Review* 8, no. 3, pp. 277–96.

Anisimova, T.A. 2007. "The Effects of Corporate Brand Attributes on Attitudinal and Behavioural Consumer Loyalty." *Journal of Consumer Marketing* 24, no. 7, pp. 395–405.

Arnolds, C.A., and C. Boshoff. 2002. "Compensation, Esteem Valence and Job Performance: An Empirical Assessment of Alderfer's ERG Theory." *International Journal of Human Resource Management* 13, no. 4, pp. 697–719.

Atkinson, J.W. 1957. "Motivational Determinants of Risk Taking Behavior." *Psychological Review* 64, no. 6, pp. 359–72.

Banerjee, S. 2016. "Influence of Consumer Personality, Brand Personality, and Corporate Personality on Brand Preference: An Empirical Investigation of Interaction Effect." *Asia Pacific Journal of Marketing and Logistics* 28, no. 2, pp. 198–216.

Bowlby, J. 1982. *Attachment and Loss: Vol. I, Attachment*, 2nd ed. New York, NY: Basic Books.

Bornstein, R.F. 2005. "Reconnecting Psychoanalysis to Mainstream Psychology: Challenges and Opportunities." *Psychoanalytic Psychology* 22, no. 3, pp. 323–40.

Burmann, C., S. Zeplin, and N. Riley. 2009. "Key Determinants of Internal Brand Management Success: An Exploratory Empirical Analysis." *Journal of Brand Management* 16, no. 4, pp. 264–84.

Caprara, G.V., C. Barbaranelli, and G. Guido. 2001. "Brand Personality: How to Make the Metaphor Fit?" *Journal of Economic Psychology* 22, no. 3, pp. 377–95.

Cardy, R.L., and T.T. Selvarajan. 2006. "Assessing Ethical Behavior: The Impact of Outcomes on Judgment Bias." *Journal of Managerial Psychology* 21, no. 1, pp. 52–72.

Carver, C.S., and M.F. Scheier. 2004. *Perspectives on Personality*. Boston, MA: Pearson Education Inc.

Cawsey, T., and J. Rowley. 2016. "Social Media Brand Building Strategies in B2B Companies." *Marketing Intelligence & Planning* 34, no. 6, pp. 754–76.

Cayla, J., R. Beers, and E. Arnould. 2014. "Stories That Deliver Business Insights." *Sloan Management Review* 55, no. 2, pp. 55–62.

Duncan, T., and S.E. Moriarty. 1998. "A Communication Based Marketing Model for Managing Relationships." *Journal of Marketing* 62, no. 2, pp. 1–13.

Dwyer, R.E. 2009. "Making a Habit of It: Positional Consumption, Conventional Action and the Standard of Living." *Journal of Consumer Culture* 9, no. 3, pp. 328–47.

Fan, A., L. Wu, and A.S. Mattila. 2016. "Does Anthropomorphism Influence Customers' Switching Intentions in the Self-Service Technology Failure Context?" *Journal of Services Marketing* 30, no. 7, pp. 713–23.

Flight, R.L., and K.K. Coker. 2016. "Brand Constellations: Reflections of the Emotional Self." *Journal of Product & Brand Management* 25, 2, pp. 134–47.

Füller, J., K. Matzler, and M. Hoppe. 2008. "Brand Community Members as a Source of Innovation." *Journal of Product Innovation Management* 25, no. 6, pp. 608–19.

Gabriel, Y. 2015. "Identity, Choice and Consumer Freedom-the New Opiates? A Psychoanalytic Interrogation." *Marketing Theory* 15, no. 1, pp. 25–30.

Guilford, J. 1973. "On Personality." In *Introduction to Personality*, ed. W. Mischel, 22–5. New York, NY: Holt Rinehart and Wilson.

Gupta, K.D. 2010. "Dynamics of Marital Roles in Consumer Decision Making: A Study of Indian Households." *Management and Labor Studies* 35, no. 2, pp. 209–25.

Ha, H.Y. 2016. "The Evolution of Brand Personality: An Application of Online Travel Agencies." *Journal of Services Marketing* 30, no. 5, pp. 529–40.

Hartley, J., and L. Montgomery. 2009. "Fashion as Consumer Entrepreneurship: Emergent Risk Culture, Social Network Markets, and the Launch of Vogue in China." *Chinese Journal of Communication* 2, no. 1, pp. 61–76.

Hayes, J.B., B.L. Alford, L. Silver, and R.P. York. 2006. "Looks Matter in Developing Consumer-Brand Relationships." *Journal of Product and Brand Management* 15, no. 5, pp. 306–15.

Hollebeek, L.D. 2011. "Demystifying Customer Engagement: Exploring the Loyalty Nexus." *Journal of Marketing Management* 27, nos. 7–8, pp. 785–807.

Hollebeek, L.D., M.S. Glynn, and R.J. Brodie. 2014. "Consumer Brand Engagement in Social Media: Conceptualization, Scale Development and Validation." *Journal of Interactive Marketing* 28, no. 2, pp. 149–65.

Hogg, M.K., A.J. Cox, and K. Keeling. 2000. "The Impact of Self-Monitoring on Image Congruence and Product Brand Evaluation." *European Journal of Marketing* 34, nos. 5–6, pp. 641–67.

Islam, J.U., Z. Rahman, and L.D. Hollebeek. 2017. "Personality Factors as Predictors of Online Consumer Engagement: An Empirical Investigation." *Marketing Intelligence & Planning* 35, no. 4, pp. 510–52.

Japhy, W. 2015. "Fantasy Machine: Philanthrocapitalism as an Ideological Formation." *Third World Quarterly* 35, no. 7, pp. 1144–61.

Jamal, A., and M. Al-Marri. 2007. "Exploring the Effect of Self-Image Congruence and Brand Preference on Satisfaction: The Role of Expertise." *Journal of Marketing Management* 23, nos. 7–8, pp. 613–29.

Jun, J.W., C.H. Cho, and H.J. Kwon. 2008. "The Role of Affect and Cognition in Consumer Evaluations of Corporate Visual Identity: Perspectives from the United States and Korea." *Journal of Brand Management* 15, no. 6, pp. 382–98.

Kaufmann, H.R., S.M. Correia-Loureiro, and A. Manarioti. 2016. "Exploring Behavioural Branding, Brand Love and Brand Co-Creation." *Journal of Product & Brand Management* 25, no. 6, pp. 516–26.

Lazarus, R.S. 1982. "Thoughts on the Relations Between Emotion and Cognition." *American Psychologist* 37, no. 9, pp. 1019–24.

Lazarus, R.S. 1991. *Emotion and Adaptation*. New York, NY: Oxford University Press.

Levitt, T. 1983. "Globalization of Markets." *Harvard Business Review* 61, no. 3, pp. 92–102.

Martinez, L.F., M. Zeelenberg, and J.B. Rijsman. 2011. "Regret, Disappointment and the Endowment Effect." *Journal of Economic Psychology* 32, no. 6, pp. 962–8.

McAdams, D.P. 1995. "What Do We Know When We Know a Person?" *Journal of Personality* 63, no. 3, pp. 363–96.

McAdams, D.P. 1996. "Personality, Modernity, and the Storied Self: A Contemporary Framework for Studying Persons." *Psychological Inquiry* 7, no. 4, pp. 295–321.

Merrilees, B., and D. Miller. 2005. "Emotional Brand Associations: A New KPI for E-Retailers." *International Journal of Internet Marketing and Advertising* 2, no. 3, pp. 206–18.

Mick, D.G. 2017. "Buddhist Psychology: Selected Insights, Benefits, and Research Agenda for Consumer Psychology." *Journal of Consumer Psychology* 27, no. 1, pp. 117–32.

Moon, J., D. Chadee, and S. Tikoo. 2008. "Culture, Product Type, and Price Influences on Consumer Purchase Intention to Buy Personalized Products Online." *Journal of Business Research* 61, no. 1, pp. 31–9.

Nisbet, R.E. 2000. *Stanley Schachter (1922–1997), Biographical Memoirs*, 78. Washington, DC: The National Academy Press.

Norman, W.T. 1963. "Toward an Adequate Taxonomy of Personality Attributes: Replicated Factor Structure in Peer Nomination Personality Ratings." *Journal of Abnormal and Social Psychology* 66, no. 6, pp. 574–83.

Northoff, G. 2008. "Are Our Emotional Feelings Relational? A Neurophilosophical Investigation of the James-Lange Theory." *Phenomenology and Cognitive Sciences* 7, no. 4, pp. 501–27.

Plewa, C., and K. Palmer. 2014. "Self-Congruence Theory: Towards a Greater Understanding of the Global and Malleable Selves in a Sports Specific Consumption Context." *International Journal of Sports Marketing and Sponsorship* 15, no. 4, pp. 26–39.

Pinheiro, M. 2008. "Loyalty, Peer Group Effects, and 401(k)." *Quarterly Review of Economics and Finance* 48, no. 1, pp. 94–122.

Rajagopal 2007. "Brand Excellence: Measuring the Impact of Advertising and Brand Personality on Buying Decisions." *Measuring Business Excellence* 10, no. 3, pp. 56–65.

Robbins, S. 1993. *Organizational Behavior*, 6th ed. Englewood Cliffs, NJ: Prentice-Hall.

Rosenbaum, M., M.L. Otalora, and G.C. Ramirez. 2017. "How to Create a Realistic Customer Journey Map." *Business Horizons* 60, no. 1, pp. 143–50.

Solomon, M.R. 1983. "The Role of Products as Social Stimuli: A Symbolic Interactionism Perspective." *Journal of Consumer Research* 10, no. 2, pp. 319–29.

Stanovich, K.E., R.F. West, and M.E. Toplak. 2013. "Myside Bias, Rational Thinking, and Intelligence." *Current Directions in Psychological Science* 22, no. 4, pp. 259–64.

Stauffere, J. 2012. "Social Brand Planning." *Journal of Brand Strategy* 1, no. 1, pp. 40–9.

Suciu, L.E., M. Mortan, and L. Lazar. 2013. "Vroom's Expectancy Theory-An Empirical Study: Civil Servant's Performance Appraisal Influencing Expectancy." *Transylvanian Review of Administrative Sciences* 9, no. 39, pp. 180–200.

Thellefsen, T., B. Sørensen, and M. Danesi. 2013. "A Note on Cognitive Branding and the Value Profile." *Social Semiotics* 23, no. 4, pp. 561–69.

Trijp, V., C.M. Hans, D.H. Wayne, and J. Inman. 1996. "Why Switch? Product-Category Level Explanations for True Variety-Seeking Behavior." *Journal of Marketing Research* 33, no. 3, pp. 281–92.

Valette-Florence, R., and V.D. Barnier. 2013. "Toward a Micro Conception of Brand Personality: An Application for Print Media Brand in a French context." *Journal of Business Research* 66, no. 7, pp. 897–903.

Vroom, V.H. 1964. *Work and Motivation.* New York, NY: Wiley.

Weston, H. 1999. *Mary Kay Cosmetics-Sales Force Incentives.* Cambridge, MA: Harvard Business School Press.

CHAPTER 5

Measuring Consumer Involvement

Overview

Consumer involvement in analyzing cognitive emotions is the principal element in developing perceptions, attitude, and behavior. There are many judgmental theories woven around the concepts of cognition and consumer behavior. This chapter addresses anchoring or focalism, and four-factor model comprising arousal, behavioral control, emotions, and critical thinking as part of the judgmental theories. Various perspectives on behavioral filters over cognitive biasness and aggressive and defensive behavior have also been discussed in this chapter. Decision making among consumers is critical to market information. This chapter also discusses critically the causes and effects of information analytics on decision making along with the perspectives of brand personality and trust. The chapter concludes with the discussion on trends in consumer behavior.

Customer Involvement and Satisfaction

Consumer perceptions play a key role in the life cycle of a brand. The role varies according to the stage in the life cycle, market situation, and competitive scenario. A company may need to influence the decision of consumers toward buying the brands they have not tested before, to invest on appealing communication strategies for creating awareness. Systematically explored concepts in the field of customer value, and a market-driven approach toward new products, would be beneficial for a company to derive a long-term profit optimization strategy over the period. On a tactical level, managers need to consider the optimum spread of customers on a matrix of product attractiveness and market coverage. This needs careful attention and application of managerial judgment and experience to measure the customer value-driven performance of the retail stores, considering the innovative sales approaches for organic products, store layouts, product displays supported with comprehensive point-of-sale information, brand information, and other loyalty parameters of the consumers. Customer-involved product development strategies are also found to be common with the firms in different industries, including Apple, Benetton, Corning, McDonald's, Nike, Nintendo, Sun, and Toyota. The customer firm, often a large original equipment manufacturer, perceives that its power may be cascaded throughout its supply base. At the basic level, cascading is a way for a customer to delegate responsibility to its suppliers.

Customer satisfaction is perceived to be a key driver of long-term relationships between retailer and customers, especially when customers are well acquainted with products and markets, and when industries are highly competitive. Technology-marketing efficiency is one of the principal factors, which influences customer satisfaction in a business-to-consumer and consumer-to-consumer context. This helps in building customer–retailer dyadic relationship. The key services indicators, which include effective communication, cross-functional teams, and supplier integration, are followed to develop long-term relationships. Customer satisfaction has long been considered a milestone in the path toward profitability of technology marketing firms. It is widely acknowledged that satisfaction leads to higher market share and stable revenues, while relationship between customer satisfaction levels and quality of customer services influences acquisition of new customers (Rajagopal 2010). The cognitive drivers that affect consumer behavior are discussed as follows:

- Social status to acquire and use specific products
- Self-esteem and personality enhancement
- To make contribution to the society and business by service as lead user and brand ambassador
- To satisfy hedonic value and self-governance
- To stay in public domain and gain social prominence by getting involved in the green products and with eco-friendly companies

Customer value in terms of satisfaction, use value, retailing practices, price, quality, and media appreciation is one of the indicators for building brand value for the nonconventional products and unfamiliar brands of a firm. The firms that evaluate the product performance of an innovative product in the given market and determine the approach for gaining competitive advantage over the traditional products may apply customer value concepts. To gain returns in the long run on the aggregate customer value, firms may need to methodically estimate the profitability associated thereof in terms of product attractiveness, volume of buying, and market share while introducing the new products in a competitive market environment. Customer-centric research aims at developing procustomer strategies to focus on better ways of communicating value propositions and delivering the complete experience to real customers. Learning about customers and experimentation with different segmentations, value propositions, and effective delivery of services associate customers in business, and help frontline employees acquire and retain customers with increasing satisfaction in sales and services of the firm.

Judgment Theories

Social judgment theory is a framework, which analyzes human judgments and their causes and effects like emotions and social acceptance. It is a meta-theory that directs research on cognitive perspective, which is how people perceive the situations. From the perspective of consumer behavior, this theory may be explained as consumers weigh every new idea and compare it with their present point of view to determine where it should be placed on the attitude scale in the mind. Upon reviewing the available choices, consumers subconsciously engage in sorting out ideas that occur instantly and perceptions are formed. The emotions attached to the perceptions drive consumer judgments. This theory therefore is also called as judgment theory. The psychophysical changes appear in consumers, when a stimulus is far away from one's judgmental anchor. Under such circumstances, a contrast effect is highly possible when the stimulus is close to the anchor. For example, consumers like to have test drive of a luxury car before they decide to buy. Consumer judgments also depend on the arousal they feel due to emotions attached in the decision-making process. Such assimilation effect happens whenever consumers are engaged in taking high value-high social status decisions. Judgment and decision making entail *normative analysis* identifying the best courses of action, in reference to the given values of decision makers, and examining actual behavior of a person through *descriptive analytics* in terms comparable to the normative analysis. The consumer judgments and decisions also depend on the *prescriptive interventions*, which help them to make better choices, and bridge the gap between the normative ideal and the descriptive reality (Baruch 2010).

Consumer judgment patterns, which emerge in the society today, have been explored in a research study revealing the various paradigms through an empirical analysis. This study enquires about truth, beauty, and justice as foundations for judgmental validity of consumers. This research thus generated a descriptive model of a cognitive process to produce credible evaluation judgments stating that credible judgments evolve through an iterative process, while the cognitive frameworks, decision protocols, and judgment methods may help consumers and manager to generate valid evidence. However, often these cognitive frameworks and decision-support variables are not sufficient to validate the consumer judgments. Consumer judgments on brand attractiveness use value. Purchase intentions are also influenced by the stakeholders' involvement and their participation during the judgment and decision-making process of consumers. The path required to generate a credible judgment is rarely linear and thus consumers attend product demonstrations and undergo trials on take-home and at in-store "do-it-yourself" platforms to gain experience. Credible judgment is based on the results of cognitive psychodynamics of consumers, peer evaluations, and digital discussions over time. Besides seeking second opinions, consumer judgments also depend significantly on self-reference criterion, cultural dispositions, need orientations, and qualities of the corporate professionals guiding consumers on their judgments and decisions (Hurteau and Williams 2014).

Drivers of decision making primarily originate on cognitive and psycho-neurological platforms in any market or business situation. Consumer attitudes play a significant role as drivers in decision making that focus on expectancy-value models during the judgment, and decision-making process. Consumer beliefs, motivation, social appraisal of decisions, cognitive process, planned behavior, and experimentation affect consumer judgments and decision-making process. The cognitive drivers largely determine and influence reasoned action and goal-directed behavior among consumers (Conner 2016). Emotions embedded in marketing appeals in judgmental contexts influence decision making, and consumers are largely driven by the personal and social emotions that are either related or independent to the decision. Emotions affect consumer decisions through cognitive appraisals, as each specific emotion is associated with a set of cognitive appraisals that drive the influence of the emotion on decision making through nuanced psychological mechanisms. From the perspectives of consumers and their purchase behavior, it has been observed that emotions embedded in marketing stimuli influence decision making through predetermined processes driven by cognitive appraisals (Achar et al. 2016). In the traditional paradigm, "anchored" judgments are typically explained because of elaborate thinking emerging out of consistent information in memory. However, due to the attitude change today caused by a wide range of choices among consumers, often the same judgments can result from relatively less thoughtful processes deriving consumer bias toward decision making (Wegener et al. 2010).

Focalism

Focalism or anchoring is a cognitive bias that describes the common human tendency to rely deeply on the *prima facie* information offered (the "anchor" for analysis and judgment) while making decisions. During decision-making process, anchoring occurs when individuals use unedited information to make primary and subsequent judgments on the subject or environment. In consumer products marketplace, companies promote events to familiarize consumers with new products, and drive their purchase intentions. Such strategy can be interpreted in the context of anchoring or focalism. When consumers experience emotions about a current or anticipated event, they tend to concentrate on the event, leaving aside related events in the past. Anchoring thus happens where consumers tend to assume that the feelings are driven by a single event in current focus without complex experiences. However, the negative effectives of anchoring can be observed in reference to the fact that consumers' assessment of reality can be easily manipulated by falsified and irrelevant information.

Anchoring among consumers is largely driven by personal and social emotions. The consumer choices on information analytics and judgments are affected by the following parameters:

- Emotions about a current or anticipated event
- Community perceptions and emotions
- Psychodynamics among peers

Focalism and consumer anchoring have associated effects of social cognition. In recent years, impairments in social cognition have shown an increasing tendency toward a possible explanation for these behavioral problems among people in general and consumers in particular. Social cognition refers to the mental capacities needed to recognize and understand the behavior of others, and to react appropriately within social situations. Consequently, often the perception of others' emotions, as observed in interpersonal actions or events, is converted into one's own experiences (Buunk et al. 2017). In addition, consumer culture also shapes basic cognition, such as attention, perception, categorization, memory, and heuristics. The differences in social orientation, among other factors, account for cultural differences in cognition while culture-specific thinking styles guide consumer judgments and decision-making processes. Interdependence on social orientation emphasizes the interconnectedness among consumers in a society, and promotes holistic thinking. On the other hand, an independent social orientation highlights the uniqueness and self-reliance of the individual in a society, and promotes analytic thinking (Ji and Yap 2016).

Four-Factor Model

The cognitive process among consumers is driven by four major determinants comprising arousal, behavioral control, emotions, and critical thinking that affect the abilities to make judgments and decisions. *Arousal* is a cognitive dynamics, which results into the convergence of stimulus-cognition-response model, and leads to physical changes. According to the James–Lange theory as discussed in the previous chapter(s), emotional experience depends on perception of bodily symptoms within a given situation. Mood states produce changes in physiological arousal as well as in cognitive activity, and cognitive changes are responsible for mood congruity. Hence, most consumer-centric companies always try to keep the consumers in a happy mood to perceive their surrounds to drive positive emotions (Bower 1981). Mood of the consumers is tuned to good aroma, music, videos, attractive demonstrations, and employees with positive attitudes in the retail and departmental stores. Mood, cognitive dynamics, and arousal have a linear relationship, and are often interdependent. Negative mood instances drive switching behavior in consumers, which often leads to permanent defection from the affected brand or company.

In reality, however, moods typically change slowly in intensity, whereas cognitions tend to be all-or-none and there is rapid change from one cognition to another. Mood, cognition, and arousal in a person are largely influenced by the endogenous factors comprising attention, learning, and active memory and retrieval system. Such triadic convergence of psychophysical elements not only drives arousal among consumers but also helps to form behavior over time. Consumers are also cognitively motivated to manage their level of arousal. It is predicted that this motivation systematically affects consumers' product preferences to enable consumers in a pleasant mood to choose products that are congruent with their current level of arousal, while those in an unpleasant mood will tend to choose products that are incongruent with their current level of arousal (Muro and Murray 2012).

Manifold information, wide range of choices, varied analytical platforms, and many derived consequences develop asymmetric behavior among consumers toward reaching judgments and decision-making process. Multiplicity of decision determinants drives consumers toward complex behavioral metrics. Therefore, in order to develop a sustainable behavior, it is necessary to develop *behavioral control* process through monitoring and evaluation of cognitive process, attributes, and affects thereof. Behavioral control refers to the control about how the cognitive dynamics move toward judgments and decision-making process. In a business environment, the behavior of a consumer is independent to any business management strategies. However, companies invest enormous resources in managing the consumer behavior. The behavioral control in business is referred to an employee, when the business has the right to direct and control the managerial activities. Often social and personal norms regulate the behavior of individuals, and attempt to streamline the thinking process and cognitive dynamics. Perceived behavioral control refers to people's perceptions of their ability to perform a given behavior. Drawing an analogy to the expectancy-value model of attitude (as discussed in the previous chapter), it is assumed that perceived behavioral control is determined by the beliefs, values, sociocultural determinants, and goals. Within consumer behavior, such decisions often involve the domains of spending and eating. Individual differences in self-control affect strategy effectiveness in the long run from the perspective of a company (Haws 2016).

The theory of planned behavior assumes that individuals choose their behavior and to make this choice an individual's attitudes, subjective norms, and perceived behavioral controls influence the individual's intentions. Some consumers, who are sure of their goals to achieve and maximize satisfaction, often filter manifold information, and streamline cognitive perceptions, emotions, beliefs, and values in order to deploy right decisions to maximize satisfaction (Caballero et al. 2007). Consumers intending to streamline their behavior against the diversities and incongruences lead to self-control cognitive analytics and uphold their priorities. Self-control may be explained as the tendency to consider the full range of potential consequences of a particular judgment, which exhibits the controls an individual has against unplanned compromises leading to potential dissatisfactions. These attributes allow an individual to be focused on intimate attachments, aspirations, values, goals, and beliefs, to reinforce the right behavior and decisions (Hirschi 2002). Consumers who fail to develop and execute controlled behavior are often discontented, attain low value for money, or fall into behavioral adversities like obsessive, compulsive, or negative behavior in consumption. Self-control is considered as one of the main contributors to consumer behaviors when multiple stimuli drive the cognitive perceptions, judgment, and decision-making process (Wolfe and Higgins 2008).

Emotions have a significant impact on the judgments of people. In a marketplace with a wide array of choices, emotions often act as a prominent driver in making decisions among consumers. Emotional intelligence requires that emotions are constituted or structured by judgments, and are commonly precise, to support the values and beliefs of consumers. An understanding of emotions thus involves an understanding of the judgments that structure them, and the differences may be very fine-grained and even exquisite (Solomon 2008). Judgments can be true or false, and judgments are usually done with an accompanying emotion. However, emotions are sometimes inappropriate. Conscious emotions are of qualitative character, but judgments might be quantitative as well.

Emotions are a kind of perception, which are of nonsensory character, though it often involves or is associated with sensory experience in one way or another supporting various judgments. Emotions activate consumers' goals and, thus, evoke certain behavioral responses that help them achieve these goals. There are four different categories of moral emotions comprising shame, guilt, embarrassment, and pride to a lesser extent, which belong to the category of "self-conscious" emotions (Tangney, Stuewig, and Mashek 2007; Martinez and Jaeger 2016). These emotions are evoked by self-reflection or self-evaluation, which affect consumer judgments. Among the aforementioned types of moral judgments, pride makes prominent association with consumer judgment as most companies attempt to drive this emotion to attract consumers toward making purchase intensions. The high emotional products are developed by identifying an emotional opportunity, developing a product strategy, and transferring the strategy into product features. Harley Davidson and Buick provoke "pride" as a persistent emotion among consumers through visual brand languages to successfully create multiple products under one brand, and drive positive consumer purchase intentions. An effective visual brand language (e.g., Unilever's Pure-Life water purifier) can drive both product development and market differentiation by creating consumer pride as emotion linked to cognitive perceptions (Boatwright and Cagan 2010).

Besides managing emotions as a driver for judgment and decision making, some consumers also carryout *critical thinking* to rationalize their decision process. Critical thinking is the intellectually disciplined process of actively and skillfully conceptualizing, applying, analyzing, synthesizing, and evaluating information pertaining to observation, experience, reflection, reasoning, and communication. Critical thinking serves as a guide to belief and action as well. It is based on intellectual values that transcend subject matter with clarity, accuracy, precision, consistency, relevance, sound evidence, good reasons, depth, breadth, and fairness, which help consumers in validating their judgment and decision-making process.

Behavioral Filters

People set objectives and approaches to accomplish goals, and accordingly develop perceptions, attitude, and behavior. In this process, people come across various choices, emotions, values, judgments, and intervening decision. The social and cultural beliefs also intervene in forming the perceptions and attitudes. In reference to consumers, decision making often appears to be complex due to various intervening cognitive perspectives and judgmental biases. Thus, consumers deploy behavior filters to bypass or control emotions, reinforce perceptions, rebuild attitude, and change behavior, to achieve maximum satisfaction through achieving goals.

During the filtering process, people may begin their exploration to determine the most significant observations, social and cultural values, biases, and judgments by analyzing the pros and cons of available options. In the process of filtering cognitive attributes, biases, judgments, information on the brands, products, and services help consumer measure the conceptual satisfaction. Companies appraise consumers about the features and benefits of the product or service that are of major concerns, and help in stimulating the buying perception. Consumers today use various digital platforms to analyze information, and research social and peer perceptions to get more of a sense about what other consumers are trying to make decision and for what reason. After developing comprehension about the cognitive elements to be filtered, consumers tend to develop sustainable judgments that help them toward committing to a certain decision taken by them. A spectator at the music concert or a buyer at the food store undergoes several cognitive conflicts in terms of biases, desires, and values that determine his state of mind and rationale associated with perceptions. However, due to the nature of cognitive complexities and interactive dynamics of people, they undergo critical introspection, and tend to respond to numerous questions to justify cognitive thinking and decision-making process. The counter attendant at a fast-food restaurant may offer several options, and then suggest that the customer might also wish to buy a hot apple cake pudding. Often irrelevant options and narrow time span to realize the rationale of options create cognitive disorders, and raise anomalies in rationalizing the contents, thinking, and making decisions accordingly. Positive personality traits, reasonable time span, and interconnected rationale to various levels of thought process can help people streamline their cognitive process filtering the biases, unwarranted information, insufficient evidences, and irrational exogenous push. Accordingly, a right judgment taken by the consumer also helps the order taker to rationalize options to offer consumers and manage sales effectively.

Trust is a collective behavior, which emerges over a period of time through the personality traits of individuals in a business community. Trustworthiness is sustained emotions resulting from the self-congruence, high perceived value, social acceptance, and positivity in cognitive dynamics. In the low-trust cultures, the interpersonal relationship remains obscure, and business dealings are largely discrete. Low trust cultures are tagged with evidences that help people to make appropriate judgments and decision. Most consumer products companies, therefore, not only provide information on brands, products, and services to consumers but also exhibit evidence on perceived values through sharing consumer experience across the geo-demographic segments. Generally, cognitive dynamics among consumers slow down due to unfiltered information, social and personal bias, and low-trust social environment (Rajagopal and Rajagopal 2006). Trust and interpersonal relationships contribute significantly in the cognitive process of consumers, and are typically catalytic for improving perceived satisfaction and experience. Trust in the source of information, self-reference, and consumer relations in the marketplace lead to commitment and a higher perceived value toward brands, products, and services. When trust is low in a cultural setting, it affects the confidence of the people, and depletes their responsiveness to the given situation. If a buyer relies on trust as a major driver for decision making, which in case not reciprocated, the company will suffer from substantial harm (Butler 1991). During the filtering process, consumers show two cognitive attributes, which are observation and self-appraisal without interrupting the motivation and objectives of the decision process.

Negative cognitive perspectives often disrupt the logical progression and rationale on various subsets of cognition like interrogation, recognition, and building trust. Such disruptions affect the vale perceptions during the cognitive judgment and decision-making process. Bad decisions can often be traced during the logical judgment process in the human brain. The reasoning, self-control, and decision making is a linear process in the brain, which is often misled if the right information is not analyzed and perceived values over the costs and benefits were not accurately weighed. However, sometimes the fault lies not in the decision-making process but in the mind of the decision maker due to specific cognitive obstacles. From small to big, decisions are sometimes challenging to consumers due to inadequate activation of logical frames in the brain parts. Consumer-centric companies thus play radical visuals, share experiences, and put consumers to experience the products or services, to streamline their cognition in the frontal lobe of brain. As consumers share more the radical experience, stimuli, and unusual information, they get higher cognitive arousal and are attracted toward making decision on the same lines. Many leisure and amusement parks like Six Flags, Disney Parks, and video game companies (Electronics Arts Inc.) share the radical experiences to motivate consumers toward decision making. The way the human brain works can sabotage the choices we make (Keene et al. 2006).

Consumers need to identify the anchoring or focal traps, and filter them to smoothen the cognitive process. During the dynamic cognitive process, the consumers can identify commonly following focal traps (Keeney et al. 2006):

- The status-quo trap biases people toward maintaining the current situation even when better alternatives exist. The resistance to trial or allow new perceptions to the formed is detrimental to the cognitive process toward deriving judgments and leading to decision making.
- The anchoring trap leads consumers to give disproportionate weight to the *prima facie* information and associated experience.

- The weak value for money trap gives the feeling of sunk cost to the consumers, which leads to dissatisfaction on their decision. This trap drives negative cognition and lowers the spirit of consumers to proceed ahead with the information on the decision process. Often such cognitive focal traps lead to dejection and abandoning the decision process.
- The confirming-evidence trap drives consumers to demand comprehensive information to support an existing liking on the brand, product, or services despite potential problems (assertion) and subdue opposing information (biasness).
- The framing trap occurs when a cognitive perspective, a goal, or a problem is incorrectly structured in the mind ignoring (knowledge bias, assertion, or cognitive dissonance) its consequences on the decision-making process. Cognitive dissonance is the state of having inconsistent thoughts, beliefs, or attitudes, relating to behavioral decisions and attitude change.
- The overconfidence and prudence traps override the cognitive process as subjects overestimate the expectancy, accuracy, and potential effects of decisions. The prudence makes people overcautious about uncertain events and their consequences.

Consumers can avoid these traps by carrying out qualitative analytics of information and overcome cognitive biases. Such actions would reduce the mental lapses and ensure that decisions are sound and reliable. A growing sophistication with managing risk, along with a nuanced understanding of human behavior and advances in technology that support and mimic cognitive processes, has improved decision making in many situations (Buchanan and O'Connell 2006).

Aggression and Defensive Theories

Human aggression is any behavior directed toward an individual, an object, a society, or an organization, which is carried out with the proximate or immediate intent to express dissatisfaction cognitively or physically, leading to the demonstration of unwillingness or cause harm. Some aversive events such as frustrations, provocations, loud noises, uncomfortable temperatures, and unpleasant odors produce negative cognition affects. The aggressive consumer behavior occurs upon accumulated dissatisfactions or deep deceptions in the interpersonal or business negotiations. Such aggressions lead to long-run effects causing permanent dejection with the objects or immediate suspension of decisions. This is a very sensitive situation leading also to peer instigation, public chaos, and cultural damage. The aggression among consumers in India flared up when the beef ingredients were found in the fries of an American fast-food chain in 2001. This issue has been manifested as it affected the social, cultural, and religious emotions of Hindu consumers. The American company, which has served more than 200 billion portions of French fries around the world, confessed to a method of using beef fat to partly fry chips before they are sent to restaurants. They were then frozen and refried on the premises using vegetable oil (Davis 2001). Negative effect produced by unpleasant experiences automatically stimulates various thoughts, memories, expressive motor reactions, and physiological responses, associated with the intention to manifest the anger or dissatisfaction. The cognitive neo-association theory assumes that cues present during an aversive event become associated over time with the cognitive and emotional responses caused by the event.

It has been observed that in multibranding, aggressive advertising and promotions, and multichannel routes to markets, expectation of consumers has increased manifold, while the ways to get total satisfaction have become discrete to most consumers. Such marketplace environment has aggravated the aggressive consumerism in today's context. Consumer personality traits have shown relations with physical and verbal aggressive consumer behaviors. Interestingly, there appears to be relatively little crossover effects of personality trait verbal aggression on actual physical aggressive behaviors. These cognitive drivers of aggressive consumer behavior often modify the personality traits and basic cognitive emotions (Aviv, Vassilis, and Lia 2015).

Defensive consumerism is based on both realistic and biased cognizance. The realistic defense is a state of mind of consumers that is built on experience, knowledge, social governance, and self-control. For example, defending the consumer behavior from all stimuli, advocacies, and promotions toward alcohol and tobacco consumption is regarded as defensive consumerism as it is based on the personality traits discussed in the pretext. Companies engaged in the manufacturing of food, beverages, household and personal products, packaging, or tobacco practice dual standard, ethically discouraging the consumption of such products but also engaging in manufacturing and promoting these products. The defensive consumerism largely emerges as personality outgrowth through self-control, self-governance, effective information analytics, and sociocultural values.

Information Analytics and Decision Making

Developing a right marketing strategy and its implementation involve making choices meticulously about whom to target as customers, what products to offer, and how to undertake related activities efficiently. The most common cause of strategic failure is the inability to make clear, explicit choices in these areas. It is very common for aggressive competitors to imitate attractive strategies but, perhaps more importantly, new strategic positions emerge continually. Successful incursions into established markets by strategic innovators such as Canon and the brokerage firm Edward Jones are based on strategic innovation proactively establishing distinctive strategic positions that are critical to shifting the market share or creating new markets (Markides 1999).

In formulating marketing strategies, it is necessary to involve all role players (such as manufacturers, quality and packaging managers, distributors, logistics and inventory managers, retailers, franchisees, etc.), and get fully acquainted with the marketplace environment. The low-involvement role players might lead to poor strategy implementation, however intensive feedback and business analysis would be helpful in shaping the next round of strategy formulation cycle filtering the weak ones. Strategists tend to use powerful drivers when referring to implementation efforts. Descriptors such as killers, confrontation, and engagement are linked with actions like conquering, blocking, tackling, and honing when discussing strategy implementation. Managers of firms should know that implementation is a critical ally in the building of a capable organization, and the use of the appropriate levers of implementation is the pivotal hinge in the development of the organization (Crittenden and Crittenden 2009).

Strategy can be defined as a rational set of time-sequenced actions aimed at gaining a sustainable advantage over competition and improving position with customers. Strategy answers *what and where* questions concerning business. It is a shared vision describing what the organization should be in the future and where it is going, not how it will get there. Strategy is the framework managing the "how" choices, which determine the future nature and direction of the organization. It focuses on accomplishing maximum and enduring positive differentiation as opposed to the competition in meeting customer values. The choices guided by strategy relate to the entire range of the organization's products or services, market, principal capabilities, growth rate, and return from and allocation of resources. Perhaps most importantly, strategies identify critical issues that are the changes, modifications, and additions to the organization's structure and systems, to its capabilities and resources, and to its information needs and management that result from setting the strategy.

Strategic marketing is a bridge between the marketing management and the marketing, and interplays with three forces in the markets—customer, competition, and corporate entities. The marketing strategy synchronizes the functional activities among the 3Cs and helps in building the distinctive strengths in the corporate houses to deliver better customer values. An effective marketing strategy should include a clear definition of market, an appropriate match between the corporate strengths and market needs and competitive performance. A good balance of these attributes would build a successful marketing strategy and justify the role of marketing in an organization.

Social information analysis, as an idea, can be applied in various scientific fields including planning and evaluation, education, business and management, public health, sociology and psychology, cognitive science, human development, agriculture, sustainability, environmental sciences, ecology and biology, earth sciences, and other physical sciences. Social information analysis can influence many of the existing concepts, theories, and knowledge in each of these fields (Cabrera, Colosi, and Lobdell 2008). In marketing and related business strategies, managers need to think ahead of competitors to keep moving from niche to market leader status. Changing the way does not automatically solve problems, issues, or crises in the business. However, social information analysis does

Table 5.1 Social information analytics and cognitive dynamics in decision-making

Thinking blocks	Determinants
Why	Cognitive reasoning, causes and original perspectives of thinking
What	About cognitive appraisal, judgments, objectives, processes and goals
Who	Self-reference, socio-cultural influence, marketplace promotions, information pools
Where	Personal environment, behavioral niche, socialization
How	Managing emotions, filtering biases, self-governance, following vogue, linear thinking, discrete and unstructured logical framework driving the cognitive process, ends and means, values, and perceptions
When	Need based cognition, initiation of desire driven cognitive process, subconscious stage, at the time of psychophysical arousal
Which	Sensitive variables, image portrayers, loyalty building strategies, and value generation

analyze about problem in the first place, and what solutions might look like. The reasons for the scientific utility and promise of social information analysis are extensive. Table 5.1 illustrates the rationale for social information analysis and the required strategies for implementing "social information analysis" approach through the creation of a "learning environment" in a given marketing place (Inelmen 2006).

Social information analysis in developing a marketing strategy is considered as a disciplined approach to promote competitive behavior of firms in a marketplace. Social information analysis is an approach that can provide a rational view of the situation, as well as the identification of approaches that are intended to produce the desired result. In order to develop a social information analysis approach in a business organization, it requires a substantial change in the organizational culture (O'Connor 1997). This approach would be helpful in resolving the various business conflicts, of which some include:

- Multiple perspectives on a situation causing dilemma over its management.
- Consumer behavior oscillates endlessly.
- A previously applied strategy seems to overshoot the goal and affect related areas of operation.

- Over time, there is a tendency to stay weak in negotiations.
- Problems in establishing procedural standards in the business operations.
- Decline in business growth over time.
- Lack of efforts in developing core competencies.
- Optimizing resources and their business application for augmenting growth in vital business indicators in the firm.

The social information analysis is usually driven by many smaller systems, or subsystems. For example, an organization is made up of many administrative and management functions, products, services, groups, and individuals. If one part of the system is changed, the nature of the overall system is often changed as well by definition. Systems theory has brought a new perspective for managers to interpret patterns and events in their organizations. An effective systems methodology lies at the intersection of the following four foundations of social information analysis (Gharajedaghi 2006):

- Holistic thinking focuses on the systems logic and process orientation in general. Reviewing the system in totality requires understanding the structure, function, process, and context at the same time. The systems approach enables connecting objects of various types to a single platform of thinking, to organize different forms of activity within the given time and space of the situation in business. One of the principal requirements of each successful system is an effective communication among different actions. Effective development of the organization can be achieved when various strategies, strategic planning, team work, and principles of organizational changes are applied. Technical aspects are combined with the aspects of behavior, personal (personal mastery and intellectual models) with conceptual ones.
- Operational thinking, which also signifies dynamic thinking, refers to the conception of the principles of systems dynamics, that is, evaluation of the multiloop feedback systems, identification of the delay effect and barriers of growth, mapping

stock and flow, and so on. The conception of these principles creates an additional value for managing organization in reference to business systems that emerge as an interdependent factor in decision making (Skaržauskiene 2010).

- Interactivity is a design of the desirable future, and a search for its implementation ways. Interactive design is both the art of finding differences among things that seem similar and the science of finding similarities among things that seem different. The distinct outputs of interactive design may lead to defining problems, identifying the leverage point, and designing solutions-ideation process.

- Interactive design is a part of critical thinking, which involves defining a problem, gathering of information for problem solution, formulating hypotheses, checking presumptions and correctness of findings, and making a solution. Interactive design offers a constant critical assessment, continuous learning and understanding of mental models. This dimension of social information analysis is based in intuitive thinking that stimulates creativity and provides an organization with a conceptual foundation to create a unique competitive advantage.

Self-referencing criterion (SRC) may be described as a process by which judgments on others are formed. It involves judging others' behavior against antecedents and experiences that are weighed on a preconceived platform of thinking. Before framing perceptions and conclusions, it would be wise to check with the people who are familiar with the culture of the host country, and perhaps debate the issues of concern on a knowledgeable base. However, the bottom line is that an international marketer should learn about the culture bypassing the blind trust on the first impressions or preconceptions, and play down self-referencing in favor of more objective information. Cultural adaptation refers to the making of business decisions appropriate to the cultural traits of the society. In other words, decision makers must ensure that native customs and conditions, and taboos, will offer no constraint to the implementation of the marketing plan.

Brand Personality and Trust

Perceived attractiveness of products, firms, and retail stores significantly influences the consumer-brand relationship development process in meaningful and predictable ways. Personality traits of a brand influence consumer opinion on the desirability of the brand as a relationship partner in the business of a firm. The quality connection between personality traits and brand association depends on the perceived attractiveness of the brand to a large extent. However, the role of attractiveness in the relationship varies across individual brand personality dimensions (Hayes et al. 2006). Human characteristics that attribute to a brand may be defined as the brand personality. Unlike a product brand personality, which typically relates to consumers and user imagery for a specific product brand, a corporate brand personality reflects the organizational values and culture and actions of all employees of the corporation (Keller and Richey 2006).

Amidst the growing competition and globalization effects, the luxury brands are affected by brand image inconsistencies across countries. With an increased frequency of consumer travel and penetration of international media, consumers expect brands to deliver the same values on a worldwide basis. This affects the brand image significantly if inconsistencies persist across brand destinations. Luxury brands attempt to establish a unique brand identity as an international fashion label for high-quality business, but sometimes company's other brand attributes are less apparent for consumers. Hence, the depth and variety of the brand is not fully understood by its customers (Matthiesen and Phau 2005). Consumer perceptions also determine the brand personality of virtual brands. E-retailing is primarily a functional activity, with preeminent roles for interactivity, web atmospherics, and navigability. However, users' perceptions of functional attributes are rooted in emotional associations, such as excitement or authenticity. Emotional brand associations can be utilized by e-retailers as benchmarks of key performance indicators to improve the brand performance (Merrilees and Miller 2005).

The concepts of brand image and brand identity are well connected as key assets to the brand performance. The identity of brand, from the perspective of consumers, is the foundation of a good brand-building program. Effective brand management encompassing brand personality is of paramount importance in reaching the overall company goals of satisfaction, loyalty, and profitability (Roncha 2008). Effectiveness of market communication can be measured by the periodical evaluations of brand and attributes of advertisements. Encompassing brand personality, is of paramount importance in reaching the overall company goals toward satisfaction, loyalty, and profitability. Companies may choose to deliver advertising in a more appealing dimension for quick cognitive reflexes of customers (Rajagopal 2007). Brand personality is one of the principal drivers of a brand identity. It is observed that, though contemporary scales of brand personality may not measure brand personality, they integrate various dimensions of brand identity of which personality is one of the dimensions (Azoulay and Kapferer 2003).

Brand identity not only augments the values of global brands but also enhances the ability of family businesses to persuade customers to make purchasing decisions based on the perceived attributes of the seller through a family-based brand system. Family-based brand identity influences competitive orientation (customer versus product) and performance of the firm in family businesses (Craig et al. 2008). Many global firms evolve their brand identity as a unique selling proposition (USP) in a specific retail category. The strong association between the brand image and trust, increasing competition, and changing consumer attitudes are considered as significant factors in realigning and positioning corporate brands of the global firms. However, there exist difficulties in aligning the visual identity of a retailing firm with its brand and market (Kent and Stone 2007).

Corporate image and reputation contribute significantly in building the brand identity. Volatility in the financial markets, bankruptcy, and frequent mergers and acquisitions among the global firms have been recognized as major challenges for firms competing in the changing environments. Thus, firms should consider building corporate reputation in relation to communication, identity, trust, and image (Omar and Williams 2006). It is also argued that self-image and brand identity congruence may be related to satisfaction in general among consumers, and it affects satisfaction of customers and brand value of the products or firms at varied levels of expectation. In the long run, such congruence can significantly influence brand preference, brand satisfaction, and purchase intentions of customers (Jamal and Al-Marri 2008). Findings of some research studies indicate that both the affective and cognitive components of corporate brand identity put forth significant influence on consumer attitudes toward the brand use, which in turn leads to more positive company attitudes and purchase intentions among consumers. It is observed that dimensions of personality also apply to the charity brands of global firms at causal and organizational levels, linking individual behavior of consumers. Charity brands have been found to assist income generation by enhancing donor understanding of an organization and what it stands for (Sargeant, Hudson, and West 2008).

The magnitude of consumer response to clearance sales is weighed in two ways—evaluative and behavioral. Firstly, consumer satisfaction with the decision process leading to the expected level of satisfaction is measured, which may be expressed as one of the many cognitive and affective responses that may result from a clearance sale. While explaining the basic concept of satisfaction with consumers' experience in arriving at purchase a decision, it has been argued that, although substantial research had been carried out on consumer satisfaction with the use or consumption of a good, little research had addressed consumers' experiences of learning about brands and product categories, or deciding which option to purchase (Westbrook, Joseph, and James 1978). Consumers often anthropomorphize brands by endowing them with personality traits, and marketers often create or reinforce these perceptions by their brand positioning. The brand management has developed to take advantage of new loyalty marketing vehicles. To build and maintain consumer loyalty, brand managers are supplementing mass-media advertising with interactive strategies, Internet communications, and other innovative channels of distribution. However, brand managers have to face more threats to their brands, especially parity responses from competitors. Brand loyalty can yield significant marketing advantages including reduced marketing costs and greater trade leverage (Aaker 1991).

In recent years, the number of car brands and models has grown rapidly in the global market. At the same time, the once vast gaps in quality, performance, safety, fuel efficiency, and amenities have all closed significantly. Although variations in quality and performance exist, strategies around styling, other intangibles, and the emotional benefits conferred on the customers provide a higher competitive advantage to an automobile brand. Marketers have long understood that consumers are influenced by the emotional connections they form with products, and with manufacturers, dealers, and other owners. The consumers attach significantly greater importance to relationship and emotional benefits than to a car's functional attributes at least when they meet minimum standards or do not fall far short of the competition. Nevertheless, those intangible benefits are the weakest links in the automakers' performance ratings (Chatterjee et al. 2002).

Thousands of people relate to brand personalities in the same way they do to human personalities. Psychological determinants that affect brands include thinking, sensation, feeling, and intuition. The maxim of successful branding strategy is to influence the way people perceive the company or product, and brands can affect the minds of customers by appealing to those four mind functions or their combinations. Some brands that have diet or organic appeal generate rational thinking in a person, and prompt logic and good sense toward healthy intakes. Others bands might appeal to the senses of smell, taste, sight, and sound such as fashion and cosmetic products. Some brands attract the emotional part of people appealing to the feelings dimension to which consumers react with feelings of warmth, affection, and belonging. Products such as Harley-Davidson motorcycles, and companies like Benetton with its global village branding, exemplify these. Some companies and products are attractive to people who intuitively feel comfortables with them, because they see these brands as an extension of themselves, which have a good fit to their personality, lifestyle, aspirations, and behavior. For example Body Shop projects its brands with an environmental approach.

Brands influence consumer decisions to buy in any of the preceding ways, or through combinations of them, sometimes with tremendous persuasive appeal. The brand-person associations can also have a more personal nature. Brands can be associated with people who use or have used that particular brand, for example, a close friend or a family member. Hence, it may be stated that consumers cultivate relationship with the brands that involve in lifestyle, gender, age, educational background, social values, and culture.

Trends in Consumer Behavior

Consumer culture, market, and consumerism are shifting rapidly alongside the advances in marketing and information technology. Companies today face increasing challenges to uncover factors driving consumer attitudes and behavior. Conventional strategies to manage consumers suffer from the limitations of outreach, technology support, and digital space. Thus, the traditional customer relation approaches have remained largely inoperable since the advancement of digital tools, and Internet-based customer support options. In the context of psychophysical analytics, there is growing interest in brain-based approaches, which enable managers to directly learn about customers' underlying thoughts, feelings, and intentions. The neuromarketing science is the growing discipline today toward analyzing the consumer behavior and linking it to the marketing strategy (Hsu 2017).

Neuromarketing utilizes brain-imaging technology, such as electroencephalography (EEG) and functional magnetic resonance imaging (fMRI) machines, to understand consumers' neurological responses to the marketing stimuli. Overruling the social bias and inaccurate answers that prevail in the contemporary market research, neuromarketing techniques provide insights into the consumer brain, which may be helpful to companies in marketing products and services effectively. However, when used incorrectly, neuromarketing can be invasive to the consumers, and the results can be easily manipulated by vendors, and may disrupt the healthy trend of market competition. Neuromarketing and neuroeconomics both involve the use of neuro-imaging tools, while neuromarketing focuses on the aspect of selling to a consumer, and addresses cognitive analytics to develop an improved product strategy or advertisement to attract consumers. The neuroimaging technology helps marketers understand the consumers' mind to find the motives, cognitive perceptions, and judgments associated with purchases (e.g., Campbell's Soup). Campbell Soup changed the label from the historic metallic spoon on a white background to a large white bowl filled with steaming soup some years back, as consumers revealed in primary neuromarketing experiments and survey that the old labels using eye-tracking, pupil dilation tests, and biometric measurements of heart and respiratory rates, sweat levels, and body postures were not effective to prompt consumer emotions. Neuromarketing research collected over half a billion data points and, upon analyzing these points through an algorithm, delineated activities within the participants' brain. This approach documented the neurological and physical responses rather than the routine nonclinical responses to the simple survey questions (Bart 2010; Glaenzer 2016).

Consumer-centric companies in emerging markets and developing economies have experienced little effect on the growth since the global recession of 2008–12. As a result, the potential markets have developed an outward orientation, and are trying to spur growth by turning to new sources of customer insight including "implicit" data such as biometrics, and "structured" batches of Big Data in reference to online behavior. However, in order to document the consumer behavior and develop appropriate behavioral strategies, the companies are also using the "unstructured" data such as social media and call-center conversations. They provide advice for rewiring the customer insight function in an organization (Barton et al. 2017). Most consumer products companies are engaged today in understanding consumer needs, desire, attention, and required motivation through crowd participation. The identity value, that is, revealing the sense of self, which consumers accrue by participating in creative crowds, gives a big leverage to the companies to understand the latent consumer behavior. Different types of crowdsourcing initiatives are explored from the perspective of value co-creation to provide managers a clear view of strategy to maximize value for consumers. (Fedorenko, Berthon, and Rabinovich 2017).

Technology platforms for social media commonly include Facebook, Twitter, YouTube, instant messaging, video conferencing, and web meetings. These and many other techno-communication collaboration and social media platforms have now become the lifestyle of people around the world. Firms are continuously exploring their way to enterprise communications and management strategies using the previously mentioned social media technology platforms. However, the efficiency of firms in using these social media applications and technologies poses a greater challenge and raises one of the several questions as how successful the companies are in navigating business changes through social media platforms. Though the efficiencies of firms in using social media applications vary, many firms encourage multiple talent and organizational elements in driving business communication effectively across consumer and peer segments. In this process firms work on creating a shared vision, gaining buy-in across locations and levels, and dealing with consumer expectations and streamlining consumer preferences in the day-to-day competition. Social networking and collaboration applications are extremely effective ways of converging forces of a business communication pyramid, comprising the bidirectional flow of information among the firm, consumers, and market players (suppliers, service providers, retailers, etc.). The convergence of communication can help firms in performing new processes together and to share experiences on the innovations, improvements, and temporary setbacks. People with common interests or related role players can form communities to learn from and support one another on the social media platforms. Social media can also help firms in cases where there is a need for creating a more collaborative culture and drive the change initiatives (Rajagopal 2013).

The digital space activities take a lead role in developing the consumer behavior today ever since social media burst upon the scene. There are following increasingly interactive ways in which Facebook might affect customers' behavior (John et al. 2017).

- Liking a brand passively and following it on Facebook make people more likely to purchase it.
- People's likes affect their friends' cognitive drive and intention toward purchasing.
- Liking on Facebook affects things other than purchasing, such as whether it can persuade people to engage in healthful behaviors.
- Boosting "likes" by paying to have branded content displayed in followers' news feeds increases the chances of meaningful behavior change.

In the 21st century, Facebook has turned as a major social tool that affects the perception, judgment, attitude, and behavior. Merely liking a brand on Facebook practically neither increases purchasing nor spurs friends to purchase more. However, supporting likes with branded content, however, can prompt a meaningful behavior change. The emergence of new information technologies has revolutionized digital ways for companies to interact and build relationships with customers. The channel–customer relationship has traditionally been managed through a push approach in communication with the hope to cultivate customer loyalty. However, emotional understandings of customers as how they feel about a product, service, or business drastically alter consumers' engagement, behavior, and purchasing preferences over time (Straker and Wrigley 2016).

The era of digital space and Big Data allows companies to connect with the emotions of consumers but the payoff for them might turn to be enormous. Nevertheless, building such connections is often more a conjecture than science. Firms can identify and leverage particular motivators, which would maximize their competitive advantage and growth as companies would proceed to inventory their existing market research and customer insight data, looking for qualitative descriptions. Such action would motivate their customer's desires for freedom, security, success, and other similar attributes. Further, companies should learn from their customers about the motivating elements that are specific or more important to the high-value group. They should then find two or three of these key motivators that have a strong association with their brand. This provides a guide to the emotions they need to connect with in order to grow their most valuable customer segment (Magids, Zorfas, and Leemon 2015).

Summary

This chapter bridges the theoretical and applied perspectives of judgment theory with different market segments, value propositions, and effectiveness of customer services in business. Discussion on judgment theories not only drives critical thinking but also directs research on cognitive perspective, which is how people perceive the situations. Consumer beliefs, motivation, social appraisal of decisions, cognitive process, planned behavior, and experimentation affect consumer judgments and decision-making process. The four-factor model comprising arousal, behavioral control, emotions, and critical thinking helps managers understand consumer behavior to develop marketing strategies for their products and services, and drive cognitive push among consumers. Knowledge on various behavioral filters discussed in the chapter would refine managerial learning process on consumer behavior, and comprehend acquaintance on aggressive and defensive behavior of consumers in the marketplace. Besides discussion on the behavioral perspectives of consumers, this chapter also lays foundation on the information analytics, brand personality, and trends in behavioral studies that encourage managers to carry out marketing decisions accordingly.

References

Aaker, D. 1991. *Managing Brand Equity*. New York, NY: The Free Press.

Achar, C., J. So, N. Agrawal, and A. Duhachek. 2016. "What We Feel and Why We Buy: The Influence of Emotions on Consumer Decision-Making." *Current Opinion in Psychology* 10, pp. 166–70.

Aviv, S., D. Vassilis, and L. Lia. 2015. "Consumer Misbehavior: Aggressive Behavior by Sports Fans." *Services Marketing Quarterly* 36, no. 1, pp. 22–36.

Azoulay, A., and J.N. Kapferer. 2003. "Do Brand Personality Scales Really Measure Brand Personality?" *Journal of Brand Management* 11, no. 2, pp. 143–55.

Brat, I. 2010. "The Emotional Quotient of Soup Shopping." *The Wall Street Journal*, February, 17. http://online.wsj.com/article/SB1000142405274870 4804204575069562743700340.html

Barton, C., L.R. Koslow, R. Dhar, S. Chadwick, and M. Reeves 2017. "How to Turn Customer Insight into Growth." *Rotman Management Magazine*, Spring, 74–80.

Baruch, F. 2010. "Judgment and Decision Making." *Wiley Interdisciplinary Reviews: Cognitive Science* 1, no. 5, pp. 724–35.

Boatwright, P., and J. Cagan. 2010, "The Emotion of Form and Touchpoints to Create It, Chapter 7." In *Built to Love*. Oakland, CA: Berrett-Koehler Publishers.

Bower, G.H. 1981. "Mood and Memory." *American Psychologist* 36, no. 2, pp. 129–48.

Buchanan, L., and A. O'Connell. 2006. "Brief History of Decision Making." *Harvard Business Review* 84, no. 1, pp. 32–41.

Butler, J.K. 1991. "Towards Understanding and Measuring Conditions of Trust-Evolution of Trust Inventory." *Journal of Management* 17, no. 3, pp. 643–63.

Buunk, A.M., J.M. Spikman, W.S. Veenstra, P.J. van Laar, J.D.M. Metzemaekers, J.M.C. van Dijk, L.C. Meiners, and R.J.M. Groen. 2017. "Social Cognition Impairments After Aneurysmal Subarachnoid Haemorrhage: Associations with Deficits in Interpersonal Behaviour, Apathy, and Impaired Self-Awareness." *Neuropsychologia* 103, no. 1, pp. 131–39.

Caballero, A., P. Carrera, D. Munoz, and F. Sanchez. 2007. "Emotional Ambivalence in Risk Behaviors: The Case of Occasional Excessive Use of Alcohol." *The Spanish Journal of Psychology* 10, no. 1, pp. 151–58.

Cabrera, D., L. Colosi, and C. Lobdell. 2008. "Systems Thinking." *Evaluation and Program Planning* 31, no. 3, pp. 299–310.

Chatterjee, A., M.E. Jauchius, H.W. Kaas, and A. Satpathy. 2002. "Revving-Up Auto Branding." *The McKinsey Quarterly* 1, pp. 134–43.

Conner, M. 2016. "Drivers of Decision-Making: Models of Consumer Decision-Making." In *Reference Module in Food Science*, ed. G. Smithers. New York, NY: Elsevier.

Crittenden, W.F., and V.L. Crittenden. 2009. "Building a Capable Organization: The Eight Levers of Strategy Implementation." *Business Horizon* 51, no. 4, pp. 301–09.

Davis, S. 2001. "McDonald's Admits Using Beef Fat for 'Vegetarian' French Fries." *The Telegraph*, May 25. (http://telegraph.co.uk/news/worldnews/asia/india/1331625/McDonalds-admits-using-beef-fat-for-vegetarian-french-fries.html Retrieved on October 09, 2017)

Fedorenko, I., P.R. Berthon, and T. Rabinovich. 2017. "Crowded Identity: Managing Crowdsourcing Initiatives to Maximize Value for Participants through Identity Creation." *Business Horizons* 60, no. 2, pp. 155–65.

Gharajedaghi, J. 2006. *Systems Thinking: Managing Chaos and Complexity*. San Diego, CA: Elsevier.

Glaenzer, E. 2016. *Are the Brain and the Mind One? Neuromarketing and How Consumers Make Decisions*. Honors Theses, Paper 812, Colby College, Waterville, ME. (http://digitalcommons.colby.edu/honorstheses/812 Retrieved on October 09, 2017).

Haws, K.L. 2010. "Enhancing Self-Control in Consumer Decisions." *Current Opinion in Psychology* 10, pp. 118–23.

Hayes, J.B., B.L. Alford, L. Silver, and R.P. York. 2006. "Looks Matter in Developing Consumer-Brand Relationships." *Journal of Product and Brand Management* 15, no. 5, pp. 306–15.

Hirschi, T. 2002. *Causes of Delinquency*. New Brunswick, NJ: Transaction Publishers.

Hsu, M. 2017. "Neuromarketing: Inside the Mind of the Consumer." *California Management Review* 59, no. 4, pp. 5–22.

Hurteau, M., and D.D. Williams. 2014. "Credible Judgment: Combining Truth, Beauty, and Justice." *New Directions for Evaluation* 2014, no. 142, pp. 45–56.

Inelmen, E. 2006. "Genealogy of a Pursuit for Education Reform." In *Philosophy of Education: Proceedings of the Twenty-First World Congress of Philosophy*, ed. D. Evans, 57–64. 4 vols. Ankara, Turkey.

Jamal, A., and M. Al-Marri, 2007. "Exploring the Effect of Self-Image Congruence and Brand Preference on Satisfaction: The Role of Expertise." *Journal of Marketing Management* 23, nos. 7–8, pp. 613–29.

Ji, L.J., and S. Yap. 2016. "Culture and Cognition." *Current Opinion in Psychology* 8, pp. 105–11.

John, L.K., D. Mochon, O. Emrich, and J. Schwartz. 2017. "What's the Value of a Like?" *Harvard Business Review* 95, no. 2, pp. 108–15.

Keeney, R.L., H. Raiffa, and J.S. Hammond. 2006. "Hidden Traps in Decision Making." *Harvard Business Review* 76, no. 5, pp. 47–58.

Keller, K.L., and K. Richey. 2006. "The Importance of Corporate Brand Personality Traits to a Successful 21st Century Business." *The Journal of Brand Management* 14, nos. 1–2, pp. 74–81.

Kent, T., and D. Stone. 2007. "The Body Shop and the Role of Design in Retail Branding." *International Journal of Retail & Distribution Management* 35, no. 7, pp. 531–43.

Magids, S., A. Zorfas, and D. Leemon. 2015. "The New Science of Customer Emotions." *Harvard Business Review* 91, no. 9, pp. 90–8.

Markides, C.C. 1999. "Dynamic View of Strategy." *Sloan Management Review* 40, no. 3, pp. 55–63.

Martinez, L.F., and D.S. Jaeger. 2016. "Ethical Decision Making in Counterfeit Purchase Situations: The Influence of Moral Awareness and Moral Emotions on Moral Judgment and Purchase Intentions." *Journal of Consumer Marketing* 33, no. 3, pp. 213–23.

Matthiesen, I., and I. Phau. 2005. "The 'HUGO BOSS' Connection: Achieving Global Brand Consistency Across Countries." *The Journal of Brand Management* 12, no. 5, pp. 325–38.

Muro, F.D., and K.B. Murray. 2012. "An Arousal Regulation Explanation of Mood Effects on Consumer Choice." *Journal of Consumer Research* 39, no. 3, pp. 574–84.

O'Connor, J. 1997. *The Art of Systems Thinking: Essential Skills for Creativity and Problem Solving*. London: Thomson Harper Collins.

Omar, M., and R.L. Williams. 2006. "Managing and Maintaining Corporate Reputation and Brand Identity: Haier Group Logo." *Journal of Brand Management* 13, nos. 4–5, pp. 268–75.

Rajagopal., and A. Rajagopal. 2006. "Trust and Cross-Cultural Dissimilarities in Corporate Environment." *Team Performance Management Journal* 12, nos. 7–8, pp. 237–52.

Rajagopal 2007. "Stimulating Retail Sales and Upholding Customer Value." *Journal of Retail and Leisure Property* 6, no. 2, pp. 117–35.

Rajagopal 2010. "Conational Drivers Influencing Brand Performance Among Consumers." *Journal of Transnational Management* 15, no. 2, pp. 186–211.

Rajagopal 2013. *Managing Social Media and Consumerism: The Grapevine Effect in Competitive Markets.* Basingstoke, Hampshire, UK: Palgrave Macmillan.

Roncha, A. 2008. "Nordic Brands Towards a Design-Oriented Concept." *Journal of Brand Management* 16, nos. 1–2, pp. 21–9.

Sargeant, A., J. Hudson, and D.C. West. 2008. "Conceptualizing Brand Values in the Charity Sector: The Relationship Between Sector, Cause and Organization." *The Service Industries Journal* 28, no. 5, pp. 615–32.

Skaržauskiene, A. 2010. "Managing Complexity: Systems Thinking as a Catalyst of the Organization Performance." *Measuring Business Excellence* 14, no. 4, pp. 49–64.

Solomon, R.C. 2008. *True to Our Feelings: What Our Emotions Are Really Telling Us.* Cary, NC: Oxford University Press.

Straker, K., and C. Wrigley. 2016. "Designing an Emotional Strategy: Strengthening Digital Channel Engagements." *Business Horizons* 59, no. 3, pp. 339–46.

Tangney, J.P., J. Stuewig, and D.J. Mashek. 2007. "Moral Emotions and Moral Behavior." *Annual Review of Psychology* 58, no. 1, pp. 345–72.

Wegener, D.T., R.E. Petty, K.L. Blankenship, and B. Detweiler-Bedell. 2010. "Elaboration and Numerical Anchoring: Implications of Attitude Theories for Consumer Judgment and Decision Making." *Journal of Consumer Psychology* 20, no. 1, pp. 5–16.

Westbrook, R.A., W.N. Joseph, and R.T. James. 1978. "Satisfaction/Dissatisfaction in the Purchase Decision Process." *Journal of Marketing* 42, no. 4, pp. 54–60.

Wolfe, S.E., and G.E. Higgins. 2008. "Self-Control and Perceived Behavioral Control: An Examination of College Student Drinking." *Applied Psychology in Criminal Justice* 4, no. 1, pp. 108–34.

About the Author

Rajagopal is Professor of Marketing at EGADE Business School of Monterrey Institute of Technology and Higher Education (ITESM), Mexico City Campus, and Life Fellow of the Royal Society for Encouragement of Arts, Manufacture and Commerce, London. Dr. Rajagopal is also Visiting Professor at Boston University, Boston, Massachusetts. He has been listed with biography in various international directories. He offers courses in the areas of marketing, innovation management, and international business to the students of undergraduate, graduate, and doctoral programs. He has imparted training to senior executives and has conducted over 65 management development programs to the corporate executives and international faculty.

Rajagopal holds postgraduate and doctoral degrees in economics and marketing, respectively, from Ravishankar University in India. He has to his credit 54 books on marketing and innovation management themes and over 400 research contributions that include published research papers in national and international refereed journals. He is Editor-in-Chief of International Journal of Leisure and Tourism Marketing, International Journal of Business Competition and Growth, and International Journal of Built Environment and Asset Management. Dr. Rajagopal is also Regional Editor of Emerald Emerging Markets Case Studies, published by Emerald Publishers, the United Kingdom. He is on the editorial board of various journals of international repute. His research contributions have been recognized by the National Council of Science and Technology (CONACyT), Government of Mexico, by awarding him the honor of the highest level of National Researcher-SNI Level-III.

He has been awarded UK-Mexico Visiting Chair 2016 to 2017 for collaborative research on "Global-Local Innovation Convergence" with University of Sheffield, the United Kingdom, instituted by the Consortium of Higher Education Institutes of Mexico and the United Kingdom. Throughout his career, Dr. Rajagopal has delivered a number of courses and executive and doctoral programs regarding the areas of marketing and international business for institutions such as the Indian Institute of Management, Indore and Rohtak, India; Narsee Monjee Institute of Management Studies, Mumbai, India; Vigyana Jyoti Institute of Management, Hyderabad, India; Institute of Public Enterprise, Hyderabad, India; International Management Institute, Delhi, India; and Boston University, Boston, MA, the United States.

Dr. Rajagopal's fields of teaching and research include marketing strategy, consumer behavior, technology and innovation management, international business administration, services marketing, new product management, and brand management. As a result of his academic excellence, the Government of Mexico has recognized him for the best executive program on innovation, technology, and competitiveness as well as the top-level researcher.

Index

OTHER TITLES IN OUR CONSUMER BEHAVIOR COLLECTION

Naresh Malhotra, Georgia Tech, Editor

- *Fashion Marketing: Influencing Consumer Choice and Loyalty with Fashion Products* by Caroline Le Bon
- *Store Design and Visual Merchandising: Creating Store Space That Encourages Buying, Second Edition* by Claus Ebster and Marion Garaus
- *Consumer Experiences and Emotion Management* by Avinash Kapoor
- *Shopper Marketing: A How-To Business Story* by Paul Barnett

Announcing the Business Expert Press Digital Library

Concise e-books business students need for classroom and research

This book can also be purchased in an e-book collection by your library as

- a one-time purchase,
- that is owned forever,
- allows for simultaneous readers,
- has no restrictions on printing, and
- can be downloaded as PDFs from within the library community.

Our digital library collections are a great solution to beat the rising cost of textbooks. E-books can be loaded into their course management systems or onto students' e-book readers.
The **Business Expert Press** digital libraries are very affordable, with no obligation to buy in future years. For more information, please visit **www.businessexpertpress.com/librarians**. To set up a trial in the United States, please email **sales@businessexpertpress.com**.

www.ingramcontent.com/pod-product-compliance
Lightning Source LLC
Chambersburg PA
CBHW060544210326
41519CB00014B/3336